The Architecture of the Universities of Leicester

Third Edition

Arthur Lyons

ANCHOR
PRINT GROUP LTD

First edition 2010
Second edition 2012
Third edition 2017

Published and printed by AnchorPrint Group Ltd
www.AnchorPrint.co.uk

ISBN-13: 978-1-910181-37-9

The Author

D r Arthur Lyons, author of texts on building materials, was formerly Head of Quality, Principal Lecturer and Teacher Fellow for construction materials and computer-aided design in the Leicester School of Architecture, Faculty of Arts, Design and Humanities, De Montfort University, Leicester, UK. He was head boy at Hawarden Grammar School, Flintshire, from where he was awarded a State Scholarship and Open Exhibition to Trinity Hall, Cambridge. Arthur Lyons studied natural sciences at Cambridge, molecular sciences at the University of Warwick and polymer chemistry at the University of Leicester where he took a PhD, followed by a two-year post-doctoral fellowship under Professor Martyn Symons in the Department of Physical Chemistry. After two years at Thames Polytechnic (now Greenwich University), Arthur Lyons took up a teaching post at the Leicester Polytechnic School of Architecture, where he studied for the postgraduate diploma in architectural building conservation. He was a lecturer in building materials and computer-aided design within schools of architecture and surveying for thirty five years. His book 'Materials for Architects and Builders' – Routledge, now in its fifth edition, is one of the standard texts for students of architecture, surveying and construction. Arthur Lyons has also made significant contributions to other key texts including the Routledge 'Metric Handbook – Planning and Design Data' and the Institution of Civil Engineers 'Manual of Construction Materials'.

In recognition of his services to architects and architecture, Arthur Lyons was honoured with life membership of the Leicestershire and Rutland Society of Architects and he is sole extant recipient of this prestigious award. A former Quality Assurance Agency auditor for higher education and current Fellow of the Higher Education Academy, he retains his active interest in architecture through liaison with the Leicestershire and Rutland Society of Architects and the Leicester School of Architecture of De Montfort University where he is an Honorary Research Fellow.

The author acknowledges the assistance of Susan Lyons, educated at Homerton College, Cambridge and a graduate of the University of Leicester, who maintains a strong and critical interest in local history. The author also acknowledges the continuing support of his daughters Claire and Elizabeth; Elizabeth holds a MA in Personnel and Development at De Montfort University.

Acknowledgements

The author wishes to acknowledge the support for this book by Professor Paul Boyle, President and Vice-Chancellor of the University of Leicester and Professor Dominic Shellard Vice-Chancellor of De Montfort University.

The assistance of the following staff and associates of the two universities has been invaluable for updating this text for a third edition. In addition, I wish to record my thanks to the Record Office for Leicestershire, Leicester and Rutland for their tremendous support.

University of Leicester:

Steve Abraham, Marketing and Student Recruitment

Kate Godfrey, Head of Public Affairs

Samantha Hirst, Executive Assistant to the President and Vice-Chancellor

Mike Queally, Former Assistant Director, Head of Estates Development

Peter Thorley, News Projects Officer

Matt Weir, Associate Director Sports Development

De Montfort University:

Susan Barton, Honorary Research Fellow

Umesh Desai, Director of Estates and Commercial Services

James Gardner, Pro Vice-Chancellor Strategic and International Partnerships

Gurpreet Johal, Corporate Marketing Officer

Chris Johnston, Senior Media Officer

Katherine Short, Archivist and Special Collections Team Manager

Colleen Thorneycroft, Estates Manager

The Record Office for Leicestershire, Leicester and Rutland, Long Street, Wigston Magna, Leicester LE18 2AH.
The views expressed are entirely those of the author and not of the two universities.
Photographs are by the author except where otherwise noted.

The author acknowledges permissions to print copyright images from the following sources.

David Wilson Clarke, Photography

De Montfort University

Gateway Sixth Form College, Colin Grundy Drive, Hamilton, Leicester LE5 1GA

Jason Senior, Redpix Photography

Leicester City Council, Planning Policy and Design Group, New Walk Centre, Welford Place, Leicester LE1 6ZG

Leicester Mercury, St George Street, Leicester LE1 9FQ

Record Office for Leicestershire, Leicester and Rutland, Long Street, Wigston Magna, Leicester LE18 2AH

Shepheard Epstein Hunter – Architecture Planning Landscape, Phoenix Yard, 65 Kings Cross Road, London WC1X 9LW

Trinity Hospital, Clerk to the Governors, 50 Western Boulevard, Leicester LE2 7BU

University of Leicester

Contents

Foreword

Foreword by Professor Paul Boyle, President and Vice-Chancellor, University of Leicester

I am honoured to have been asked to write a foreword for this – new and updated – version of The Architecture of the Universities of Leicester. I am happy to do so, as the previous edition, introduced by my predecessor Professor Sir Bob Burgess, has been an invaluable companion to a generation of our students and academics.

University life is in constant flux, as new groups of students embark on their studies every year and other groups leave to join the world of work. Less often considered is that our campus is also constantly evolving, as we invest in new facilities and adapt the university's existing buildings to new modes of learning and discovery.

In the years since the first publication of 'The Architecture of the Universities of Leicester' our campus has seen a programme of continued development and rehabilitation which is continuing now. With some of our most famous building stock completed in the 1960s, there are inevitably problems of wear and tear and we are now revitalising these parts of the estate. A £20m investment is now allowing us to replace the 2,500 tilted glass panels that make up the roof of the Engineering building. This unique building holds a place in architectural history, earning a rare place on a stamp, and it is essential that we secure its future well into the 21st century. Interestingly, the height of this building was determined by the head of water required for thermofluids and hydraulics experiments. To this day, 11th floor water tanks supply hydraulic pressure to ground floor labs via enormous pipes which run down the main staircase.

At the start of 2017 we are unveiling our new public space at the heart of campus. Previously a carpark (and in the light of our discovery of Richard III, the university hears a lot of jokes about our fondness for carparks), the new square will turn the orientation of the university inward, creating a new central hub, and a public resource for staff, students and for the broader communities who share our facilities.

Elsewhere, we have seen consistency of theme if not building style. Throughout our hundred year history, the University of Leicester has become known for championing new architectural approaches. We expect all of our buildings to contribute to the university's strong record for sustainability and environmental performance. Our most recent building – the Centre for Medicine (CfM) – is another pioneering commission as it is the largest non-residential PassivHaus construction in the UK. The unique 'fabric first' design of the CfM helps to reduce energy costs by 80%.

We understand – and value – the place of our buildings as part of Leicester's heritage; but above all, we regard our campus practically, as the place where we fulfil Leicester's mission to research and to teach. We are very proud of our estate and trust that our staff, students and the wider public will value it for generations to come.

Foreword

Foreword by Professor Dominic Shellard, Vice-Chancellor, De Montfort University

The quality and character of De Montfort University's (DMU) buildings provide a source of both pride and inspiration. Some send strong signals about the values and vision of a shared past, while others re-state the university's continued confidence in the future.

The Magazine dates from the 15th century; Trinity House, where I write this, contains elements of an original 14th-century structure. Arches from Leicester's Church of the Annunciation, to which the battle-scarred body of Richard III was carried from Bosworth, form the centrepiece of our Heritage Centre, and we are creating the ultra-modern Leicester Castle Business School in the Grade 1 listed Great Hall of an important 11th-century stronghold.

The challenge and excitement of that venture have also informed our vast and ambitious campus transformation, now nearing completion. When I became the Vice-Chancellor of DMU, it was clear we needed to reaffirm our purpose by investing to provide the outstanding buildings and facilities our students deserve and demand. So we set about creating just such buildings and facilities, set alongside a green swathe through what I believe is the finest city centre campus in Britain. All will become part of our cultural and architectural heritage.

The centrepiece is the Vijay Patel Building. It holds sector-leading facilities for students on our Art and Design courses, but its spirit of excellence and adventure is one shared across all faculties and disciplines, and its signature tower is an encouragement to us all to look higher and to stand out.

Students come to DMU to gain the skills that allow them to express themselves meaningfully in the working world, none more so that those with a passion for Architecture. Leicester School of Architecture was established in 1897, making it one of the oldest in the UK, and our graduates have gone on to careers with leading practices in the UK and overseas, and in related fields such as architectural conservation, urban design, research, planning and project management. DMU is a UK top 30 Architecture course, according to the Sunday Times Good University Guide 2016; Architecture at DMU is ranked in the top 10 for research quality. DMU talent will literally help to build the future.

That will please greatly former lecturer Dr Arthur Lyons, whose excellent book here adds immeasurably to our wider understanding and appreciation of a great and still-unfolding story. I know you will enjoy it as much as I did.

**DE MONTFORT
UNIVERSITY
LEICESTER**

Introduction

Leicester is fortunate in having two prestigious universities each with their own characteristic campuses featuring buildings of national and international repute. The two universities are broadly complementary in their teaching and research portfolios. The University of Leicester, founded in the early twentieth century, offers a broad spread of academic disciplines underpinned by a strong research base. De Montfort University, dating back to the late nineteenth century through its constituent colleges, focuses on the professional, vocational and creative disciplines. This book is intended to illustrate the architectural features of the key buildings on each campus, indicating their brief histories and current academic use. It is hoped that the text will be of interest to students and alumni of both universities who relate their undergraduate and postgraduate experiences both to specific buildings and to their whole campus including the social and library facilities. The book will also be of interest to local history groups.

It is an interesting coincidence that both universities are sited on former asylum locations! Furthermore, the key benefactor, Thomas Fielding Johnson JP, who donated the original site and buildings for what is now the University of Leicester, lived for forty five years in Brookfield House, which was the central building of the former De Montfort University's Charles Frears campus and is now part of the University of Leicester's estate as Brookfield.

Today we see the two institutions as distinct universities in their own right; however, back in 1930, Councillor C.R. Keene had proposed some form of co-ordination between the work of the Leicester Colleges of Art and Technology and the University College, but this was firmly rejected by the University College Council. The idea of affiliation was again raised in 1949, but this time it was the University Grants Committee who settled the issue by intimating that it would not fund the plan.

The Queen has honoured each university by two visits. In May 1958, she officially opened the Percy Gee Building of the University of Leicester, and in December 2008, Her Majesty officially opened the new University Library. In December 1993, Her Majesty opened and named the Queen's Building of De Montfort University and in March 2012, Her Majesty The Queen, accompanied by HRH The Duke of Edinburgh and HRH The Duchess of Cambridge, commenced her Diamond Jubilee celebrations with a visit to De Montfort University Magazine Square and the Hugh Aston Building. Both universities hold national Centres for Excellence in Teaching and Learning. The University of Leicester has three, namely; the Department of Physics and Astronomy - Innovative Physics Teaching, the Department of Genetics - Genetics Education Networking for Innovation and Excellence, and the Department of Geography – Spatial Literacy in Teaching. De Montfort University has the Centre for Excellence in Performing Arts within the Faculty of Arts, Design and Humanities.

The buildings on the two main university campuses are listed in date order, whilst noting the separate campuses of the University of Leicester. The third edition of the text includes buildings and development plans to 2016, and removes buildings described in previous editions which are no longer part of the University of Leicester or De Montfort University's estates.

The Clock Tower, Leicester – 1868

The University of Leicester

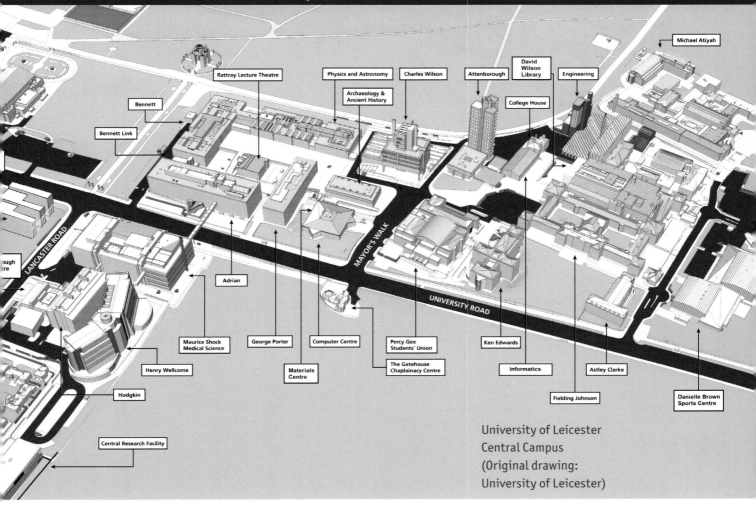

University of Leicester
Central Campus
(Original drawing:
University of Leicester)

The University of Leicester campus is situated to the south-east of the city centre adjacent to the Victoria Park with its associated Edwin Lutyens pavilions (1933) and war memorial (1923), also the De Montfort Hall (1913) used for graduation ceremonies. To the city side of University Road is the 30 acres (12 hectares) of the Welford Cemetery (1849), designed by J.R. Hamilton and J.M. Medland as a park, although currently the densely planted perimeter acts as a visual barrier from the University.

The campus has developed by extension along and across University Road and down Lancaster Road towards the city. The Leicester Medical School has space embedded within Leicester's three major hospitals, including the Robert Kilpatrick Building Clinical Sciences Building (1978) at the Leicester Royal Infirmary and the British Heart Foundation Cardiovascular Research Centre (2014) at Glenfield Hospital. Some smaller units are located in fashionable Victorian houses off Salisbury Road, Regent Road and adjacent thoroughfares. Modern University residences are located near the main campus including the Freemen's Common site, whilst the Oadby Student Village consists of modern additions to elegant Edwardian houses set in extensive gardens which also incorporate the University Botanic Garden. The official residence of the President and Vice-Chancellor, Knighton Hall, dates mainly from the early eighteenth century, and is near to College Court, designed by Sir Leslie Martin and Trevor Dannatt in 1957 as a hall of residence and upgraded to a conference and events venue in 2013. The University has an impressive legacy of buildings from the twentieth century designed by four RIBA Gold Medal winners (Leslie Martin 1973, Denys Lasdun 1977, James Stirling 1980 and Philip Dowson (Arup Associates) 1981). The university buildings support the academic functions of the three colleges, namely Social Sciences, Arts & Humanities; Medicine, Biological Sciences & Psychology and Science & Engineering.

Environs of the University of Leicester

University from the adjacent Victoria Park opened to the public in 1883

De Montfort Hall – Designed by Shirley Harrison in 1913

Shirley Harrison was the son of the architect Stockdale Harrison who worked in Leicester from 1870 and subsequently set up the practice Stockdale Harrison and Sons with his two sons, Shirley and James.

Victoria Park Lodges and Gates – Designed by Sir Edwin Lutyens in 1931-33

War Memorial – Designed by
Sir Edwin Lutyens in 1923

Victoria Park Pavilion
and Clock Tower – 1958

Welford Road Cemetery – Designed by
Hamilton and Medland
and opened in 1849

Fire Station, Lancaster Road –
Designed by A.E. & T. Sawday
in 1927

The local architectural practice
was founded in 1878 originally as
Redfern & Sawday. Albert Edwin
Sawday was Mayor of Leicester
in 1903.

New Walk

New Walk was laid out by the Corporation, originally as Queen's Walk, in 1785. Originally as a path through open fields, it was planted with trees and hedges, but after 1804, gradually the adjacent streets were laid out and from 1824, New Walk itself was slowly developed. New Walk was designated as Leicester's first Conservation Area in 1969. Heritage Lottery Funding in 2002 launched a programme to restore much of New Walk to its 19th century appearance.

St James the Greater – Designed by Henry Langton Goddard in 1899

St James the Greater was designed by Goddard & Co., a practice which eventually spanned six generations of architects in Leicester. The building was not completed until 1914, and then with the planned tall west tower replaced by a brick and stone pedimented façade.

'Tuscan Landscape' by Ken Ford, 2002

Both the University Campus and the Botanic Garden are enhanced by several permanent pieces of sculpture.

De Montfort University

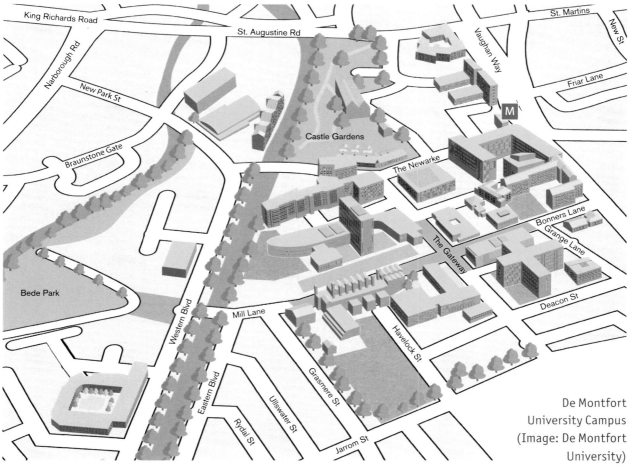

De Montfort
University Campus
(Image: De Montfort
University)

De Montfort University campus is located close to the city centre, in the historic area which includes the medieval Magazine and Turret Gateway, the Norman St Mary de Castro Church, the Newarke Houses Museum, Castle Mound and the River Soar waterfront. Some buildings are modern, whilst others have their roots in the manufacturing, social and religious history of the City of Leicester. Many of the residences associated with the University surround the campus including those on the Bede Island riverfront. The university buildings support the academic functions of the four faculties, namely Arts, Design & Humanities; Business & Law; Health & Life Sciences and Technology.

The original Leicester Art School was founded in 1870, and this was then joined by the Technical School in 1897 when the first campus building was completed. Subsequently Leicester Polytechnic was formed in 1969 through the amalgamation of the Leicester College of Technology and the Leicester College of Art, and it was established as a corporation in 1989. The institution adopted the name De Montfort University on receiving its charter in 1992. Simon de Montfort, 6th Earl of Leicester (1208 – 1265) was a distinguished figure in English history and is widely credited with pioneering representative government, the precursor to our parliamentary democracy.

The University developed with a new campus at Milton Keynes in 1992, and in 1994 merged with the Bedford College of Higher Education, the Lincolnshire College of Art and Design and the Lincolnshire College of Agriculture and Horticulture. In 2001, the Lincoln sites merged to form part of the University of Lincoln and in 2006 the Bedford campus joined with the University of Luton to form the University of Bedfordshire. The Milton Keynes campus closed in 2003 and is now part of the adjacent Open University. The Leicester Scraptoft campus, formerly the College of Education, closed in 1993 and the Grade II listed Scraptoft Hall has been converted into apartments with the grounds developed for housing. The Charles Frears campus, formerly the School of Nursing and Midwifery, closed in 2011 and was sold to the University of Leicester when De Montfort University completed the consolidation of all its programmes and research onto the city campus.

Environs of De Montfort University

Magazine Gateway –
circa 1410

St Mary de Castro –
The 1783 spire was removed
in 2013 as the structure had
become unsafe.

St Mary de Castro –
The north door, late 12th century

Skeffington House – circa 1600
The Newarke Houses Museum

Turret Gateway – 1422 - 3

Castle House – 1446 with 18th century additions

Soar River and Canal,
Mill Lane Bridge
Designed by Gimson in 1890.
The bridge abutments are
decorated as the Roman Agora
'Tower of the Winds' in Athens.

The Mile Straight –
the canalised section
of the River Soar

De Montfort University is located
close to Castle Gardens which afford
a tranquil location near to the heart
of the city.

Castle Gardens
Laid out in 1926, Castle Gardens
incorporate Castle Mound; originally
a 15m high Norman 'motte', which
would have been surmounted by
a wooden stockade, prior to the
construction of a stone castle.

University of Leicester
Campus Development Plans

The idea of establishing a university in Leicester dates back to the late nineteenth century, when it was noted by the Leicester Literary and Philosophical Society that other important English cities, including particularly Nottingham, were founding university colleges. The matter rested for three decades until it was raised again by Dr Astley V. Clarke in a presidential address to the Literary and Philosophical Society in 1912. The war intervened but the suggestion came forward in 1917 in the local press, that a lasting memorial to the war dead would be 'a university college, the stepping stone to a university itself'. It was proposed, and welcomed locally, that when the war was over the old asylum building should be used for this purpose. This effectively became the first 'campus plan'.

The asylum buildings and 37 acres were bought by Mr Thomas Fielding Johnson, who appointed trustees including Dr Astley Clarke to ensure that the asylum buildings within six of the acres became the college site. The Georgian building opened to its first students on 4 October 1921, with staff appointed to teach Botany, Geography, French, English and Latin for students preparing for the University of London Intermediate examination. Subsequently, in 1924, unoccupied sections of the original building were modified for physics and chemistry.

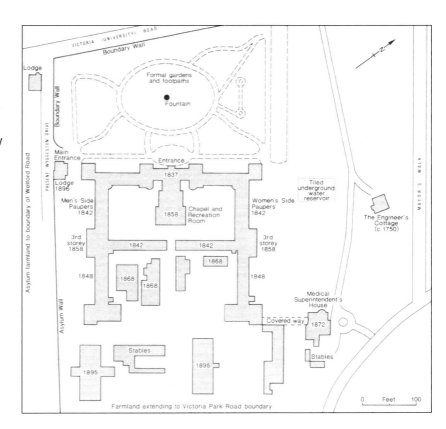

The Buildings of the Leicestershire and Rutland County Lunatic Asylum (Drawing: Leicestershire's Lunatics, H.G. Orme and W.H. Brock)

UNIVERSITY COLLEGE LEICESTER
DEVELOPMENT PLAN

FUTURE BUILDINGS
University Road

CHEMISTRY BUILDING

Mayors Walk

STUDENT'S UNION BUILDING

Biological Science Wing

war memorial

Proposed future Extension

Wyggeston Grammar Sch (boys)

boundary of College property

Block Plan
Scale . 1/2500 th

Thomas Worthington & Sons architects

In 1945 the University Grants Committee, motivated by a need to expand the number of student places after the war, agreed to recommend the College for financial assistance from the Exchequer. In view of the anticipated expansion, the College, despite some local opposition, successfully completed negotiations for the purchase of an additional nine acres of sports grounds to the north-east side of Mayor's Walk from the City Council. About this time Knighton Hall (a mile from the campus) was purchased and became the Principal's official residence, leaving College House, the original asylum Medical Superintendent's house, for additional female student accommodation. As numbers rose, the proportion of non-local students increased, so the need for male residences became imperative. The College Council accepted that student accommodation and academic buildings would necessarily be on separate locations. The Council therefore purchased three Jacobean-style houses, Netherclose (1902 - now Hastings House), Middlemeade (1908 - now Beaumont House) and Sorrento (1906 - now Shirley House) in Oadby, each with large gardens with the potential for further development.

The first significant new building work on the campus came with the closing off of the major quadrangle, to complete the rectangle of the original 'main' building between the two rear 1848 wings. The work was commissioned from the University architect William Keay of Pick Everard Keay and Gimson

and spanned three years from 1948 to 1950. However, it was generally agreed that the poor materials used, due to post-war shortages, destroyed the architectural unity of the old building. In 1958, Professor Jack Simmons, the eminent historian, noted that there was no point in opening up the whole large quadrangle interior to expose the unworthy extension of 1950. This extension to the main building was removed for the construction of the first phase of the library which was completed in 1974.

When it was clear that the original 'main' building could

Campus Development Plan by Shirley Worthington, 1947 (Drawing: University of Leicester Archive) no longer accommodate the full range of academic activities, the College appointed Messrs Thomas Worthington & Sons of Manchester as Consultant Architects to draw up plans for the development of the whole campus. The architectural practice had been established in 1849, and by the mid-twentieth century was headed by Hubert Worthington, although it was his nephew, T. Shirley Worthington who was most involved in the Leicester project. The practice had built in Manchester, Oxford and London including university buildings and had an appropriate pedigree based on sound classical architecture. By 1947, the practice had developed a campus master plan which extended through a series of symmetrical quadrangles beyond Mayor's Walk to the war memorial.

The plan was intended to empathise stylistically with the Fielding Johnson Building by the use of subdued classical architecture and

local buff bricks. It had always been the intention, according to Professor Jack Simmons, that the front lawn should be kept as a 'precious asset', and this remains today. The Worthington campus plan, which included the Astley Clarke Building completed in 1951, and the Percy Gee Building completed in 1958, was a key instrument supporting the successful bid for full university status which was granted in 1957. However, the era dominated by the Worthington architectural practice was about to close.

Following a review in 1956 of other new university buildings in England, the Council and Senate, proposed that a Consultant and Planning Architect be appointed to advise on the development of the main campus and all sites owned by the College. It was clear that senior academics and Council members, anticipating the University Charter, were seeking

Campus Master Plan by Leslie Martin, 1957 (Drawing: University of Leicester Archive)

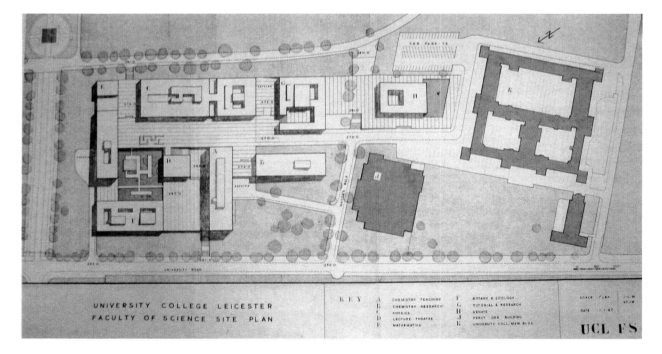

UNIVERSITY COLLEGE LEICESTER
FACULTY OF SCIENCE SITE PLAN

KEY   A   CHEMISTRY TEACHING   F   BOTANY & ZOOLOGY
       B   CHEMISTRY RESEARCH   G   TUTORIAL & RESEARCH
       C   PHYSICS   H   SENATE
       D   LECTURE THEATRE   J   PERCY GEE BUILDING
       E   MATHEMATICS   K   UNIVERSITY COLL MAIN BLDG

UCL FS

a more modern architectural style for the next phase of the campus development. A 'more adventurous architect', 'red brick and glass' and 'buildings along the top of the hill in contemporary style' were the order of the day to characterise a modern university. Professor J. Leslie Martin, Chair of Architecture at Cambridge and formerly Chief Architect to the London County Council was appointed. Leslie Martin was a prominent figure having led the design team for the Royal Festival Hall in London, and he ran his own practice in parallel with his academic commitments to Cambridge University.

In many ways Leslie Martin's 1956 scheme was not profoundly different from that of Shirley Worthington. The underlying philosophy was to create a 'collegiate atmosphere' with the built form creating

enclosures, with the suggestion of quadrangles, very familiar to Leslie Martin in Cambridge. The contemporary low-rise buildings would be built in local brick to give continuity with the older campus buildings, but would capitalise on the natural changes in level to create enclosures and interesting views. The Master Plan, to be built in stages, sought to retain the view of the city from Victoria Park, without diminishing the importance of the Lutyens War Memorial. The revised plan of 1957 (illustrated) incorporated a two-storey Senate House, located where the Charles Wilson was subsequently built.

The first proposals were for new Chemistry and Physics buildings, also a new hall of residence, College Hall, on the Knighton site. This was quickly followed by the Bennett building for Mathematics, Geology and Geography which formed the

Royal Festival Hall,
London, 1951 –
Designed by Sir Leslie Martin
and refurbished in 2008
by Rick Mather with
Allies & Morrison

CHEMISTRY RESEARCH   CHEMISTRY TEACHING   PHYSICS

enclosure of the Leslie Martin courtyard.

When the Lancaster Boys School made its long-anticipated move to a new site in Knighton Fields Leicester, the University was able to acquire the extra land, on which the Engineering Building was subsequently built.

Off the main campus, Vaughan College, originally founded in 1862 as an independent adult education college, for financial reasons in 1930 became integrated with the University College. It is now within the University as the Vaughan Centre for Lifelong Learning.

Leslie Martin's Master Plan, with its focus on low-rise, low impact architecture, strongly influenced by local materials including grey-buff and yellow brickwork, was quite suddenly abandoned in the 1960s. The character of the campus which had gently evolved from its original Georgian building through the stewardship of Keay, Worthington and Martin was overturned by the Stirling and Gowan design for the Engineering Building. This was

despite the fact that it was Leslie Martin who had been instrumental in the appointment of Stirling and Gowan. Two further towers followed, designed respectively by Lasdun and Arup Associates, yet another two were planned but never realised. This new wave of development signalled the University of Leicester's determination to be seen as a modern and innovative national institution, no longer tied to the City of Leicester, but operating on the international scene. The inspiration to commission works by pioneering architects undoubtedly raised the profile of the University at a critical period in its development and still resonates today. The University is internationally acclaimed architecturally for its James Stirling Engineering Building. In 1963, Leslie Martin resigned as architect to the University over a difference of opinion relating to the university's requirement to enlarge the proposed Adrian Building above the massing envisaged in the Master Plan.

In 2002, the University commissioned Shepheard Epstein

Constructing the first buildings to the north of Mayor's Walk (Photograph: The University of Leicester, Brian Burch – printed from the Leicester Mercury)

Hunter to prepare a Development Plan, particularly noting that much of the central campus was by then thirty years old. The plan was to take a strategic view identifying all opportunities for improvement and gradual expansion of the campus over the subsequent thirty years. Key developments suggested were the provision of a new façade to the University along University Road together with a new square as the main entrance to the campus. In addition a further landscaped central square with social, catering and teaching facilities, and a new entrance square to the campus from Victoria Park were proposed. It was suggested that in the long-term the Attenborough Tower could be converted to student accommodation. The proposed additional and upgraded library provision in the 2002 Development Plan was completed in 2008.

The 2002 Development Plan also reviewed potential improvements to the North Campus, Vaughan College and the Oadby Halls of Residences, particularly focussing on pedestrian networks and accessibility. It was proposed that the South Campus (Freemen's Common and Nixon Court) should be completely redeveloped for academic and teaching use.

The subsequent Development Framework Plan 2008 also by Shepheard Epstein Hunter, was adopted by the University. The plan proposes a strategy for the next ten to twenty years, considering potential for development within the existing university estate and noting potential opportunities for extending the landholding. The architects confirmed that it would consolidate the character of the University's central site as a compact urban campus set in parkland.

Campus Development Plan, 2002
(Image: Shepheard Epstein Hunter)

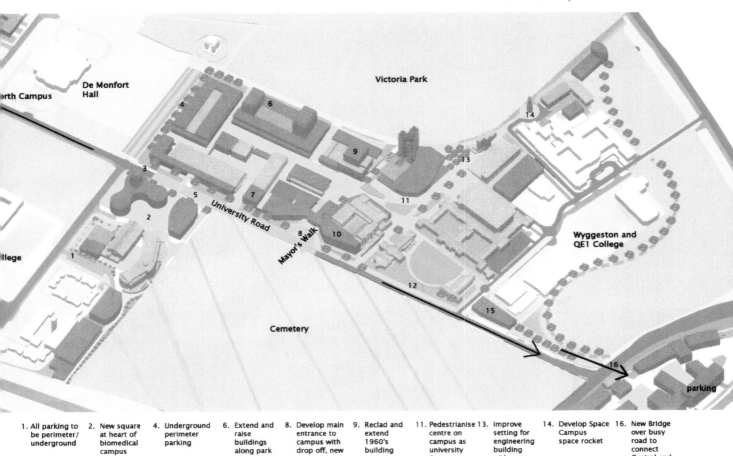

| 1. All parking to be perimeter/ underground | 2. New square at heart of biomedical campus | 4. Underground perimeter parking | 6. Extend and raise buildings along park edge | 8. Develop main entrance to campus with drop off, new entrance building and visitors' car park | 9. Reclad and extend 1960's building | 11. Pedestrianise centre on campus as university Square | 13. Improve setting for engineering building with new square at entrance to park | 14. Develop Space Campus space rocket | 16. New Bridge over busy road to connect Central and South campuses |
| | 3. New gateway buildings at campus entrance | 5. University Road as 'shared space' pedestrian priority | 7. Extend frontage to road | | 10. Extension to Student Union | 12. Open up views of listed building | | 15. New gateway building at entrance to campus | |

Campus Development Plan, 2008
(Plan: Shepheard Epstein Hunter)

The development plan suggested that the existing campus could be enhanced by the creation of a linked series of well-designed squares, defined by the buildings around them. Additional tall buildings, carefully located within the campus, could enhance the quality of the university environment and the surrounding landscape. Buildings near to the perimeter of the campus could be extended to that limit, and open spaces should have pedestrian priority by removal of most car parking areas, except for disabled persons and visitors.

A potential enhancement would be a new Mayor's Walk entrance building linked to the Percy Gee Students Union Building, leading to a podium to the base of the Attenborough Building, which would act as the focal point at the heart of the University campus, and would also define the route through to the library and Victoria Park.

Campus Development Plan, 2008 – Campus Entrance Building
(Model images- Photography: Peter Durant, Architect: Shepheard Epstein Hunter)

The Development Framework Plan also made suggestions for the enhancement of other individual buildings on the Central Campus, in particular expansion where appropriate, also the enhancement of their entrance spaces.

A major anticipated development was an extension to the Attenborough Arts Centre to create a new gallery and education space together with an outdoor court for the display of contemporary sculpture. This objective was realised in 2016.

Proposals in the university's 2015 Strategic Plan included a major investment in medical education from which the new £42m Centre for Medicine developed and the creation of a National Space Park adjacent to the existing National Space Centre. This latter new development would drive innovation in space and earth observation science, revitalise a significant section of Leicester's riverside and attract high-tech companies to the city.

De Montfort University
Campus Development Plans

De Montfort University commissioned Livingston Eyre Associates, Landscape Architects, to develop a 'Master Plan' for the campus in 1992, and this was followed by the 'Master Plan One' developed by Robert Turley Associates, Consultant Chartered Town Planners, in conjunction with the University Estates Department in 2002. Master Plan Two was produced in 2007 as development of Master Plan One by AIMS – Asset & Infrastructure Management Solutions and in 2014 Turley Associates produced the current Master Plan Three.

In more detail the 1992 'Master Plan' proposed a major development of the junction of Oxford Street and The Newarke. This was achieved by the realignment of Oxford Street to the city side of The Magazine. Work proposed to stabilise the listed remains of the former St Mary's vicarage after its partial demolition in 1947 was completed and the building is now the Square Mile Hub. The Master Plan proposal for the riverside development as a green space linking Mill Lane and

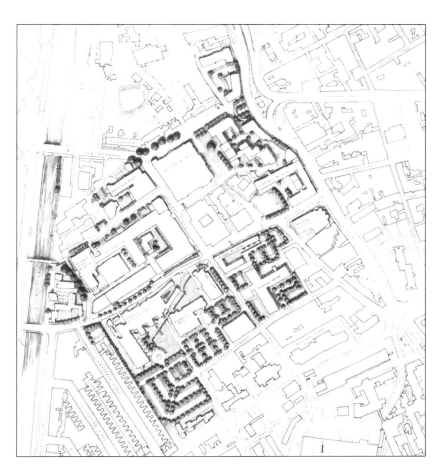

Campus Master Plan, 1992
(Drawing: Livingstone Eyre Associates)

The Newarke has essentially been realised after the closure of Mill Lane to road traffic followed by a major hard and soft landscaping scheme.

The philosophy of Master Plan One in 2002 was to 'provide a coherent

Campus Master Plan, 1992
(Drawings: Livingstone Eyre Associates)

strategy for the development of the city campus, as a benefit both to the City and the University.' High on the agenda was the formulation of a visual identity for the campus incorporating a network of attractive streets and squares within city scale quality buildings.

Master Plan One focussed on regeneration of the campus to create a lively mixed use city quarter. This included the development of additional student housing, upgraded teaching facilities, private sector developments and mixed-use street level activities. The proposal to landscape the area of Magazine Square in front of the Newarke Houses Museum to reflect the urban character of the historic space has been successfully accomplished, but the anticipated use of the Magazine archway as an entrance to the campus was not possible due to road traffic constraints. It is fortunate that the proposed commercial development at the waterfront on the site of the former William Rowlett Hall of Residence did not materialise as this has enabled the river front to become a significant feature of the university campus. Master Plan One reaffirmed that new buildings were to be located at the front of the campus, including the site where the James Went Building (1966-1973) was demolished in 2000 and this led to the construction of the Centre of Excellence in Performing Arts and the Hugh Aston buildings. Gateway Square, adjacent to the former Gateway College, has been reconfigured as proposed, but the diagonal landscaping link across to the Queen's Building is currently on hold.

Magazine Square -
Master Plan One, 2002
(Drawing: Robert Turley Associates)

Waterfront - Master Plan One, 2002
(Drawing: Robert Turley Associates)

Gateway Square - Master Plan One, 2002
(Drawing: Robert Turley Associates)

Following from the 2002 Master Plan One the University commissioned AIMS (Asset & Infrastructure Management Solutions) to develop Master Plan Two, and this was published in June 2007. This plan followed on directly from the Master Plan One. It emphasised the need to connect the university to both the city centre and the river through pedestrian friendly streets whilst picking up on the historic aspects of the campus. A key change from the Master Plan One was to develop a new art and design building on the waterfront site, previously identified for private housing and commercial development. This has been achieved with the opening of the Vijay Patel Building. The proposal for a new student sports centre materialised with the

Master Plan Two, 2007
(Plan: Asset & Infrastructure Management Solutions)

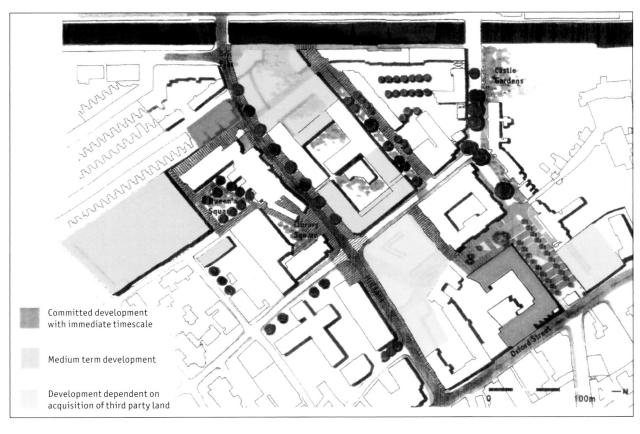

Committed development with immediate timescale

Medium term development

Development dependent on acquisition of third party land

completion of the Queen Elizabeth II Diamond Jubilee Leisure Centre.

The Master Plan Two proposal to create a diagonal pedestrian route from the remodelled Magazine Square, through Hawthorn Square and Gateway Square across Mill Lane and to a new square enclosed by the library and the Queen's Building has been modified by the retention of some of the former Gateway College buildings and the pedestrianizing of Mill Lane as the core route through the campus.

Magazine -
Master Plan Two, 2007
(Drawing: Asset & Infrastructure
Management Solutions)

Master Plan Two, 2007
(Plan: Asset & Infrastructure
Management Solutions)

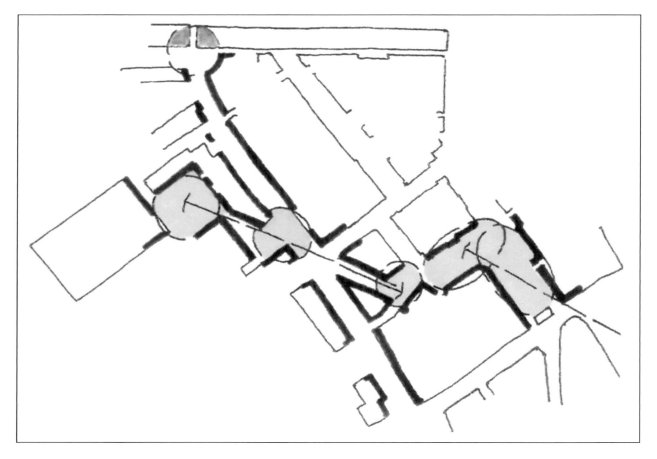

Master Plan Three reaffirmed the requirement for smooth movement of pedestrians and cyclists through the campus, but it differed from Master Plan Two as it was clear that a more logical route through the campus was from Magazine Square down the pedestrianised Mill Lane to the waterfront connecting with Bede Park on the west side of the river. This would capitalise on the new public space developed in front of the Vijay Patel building. This work has been completed so there is now a clear and safe route between the city and Bede Island. The café overlooking the river adds to the vibrant city centre campus.

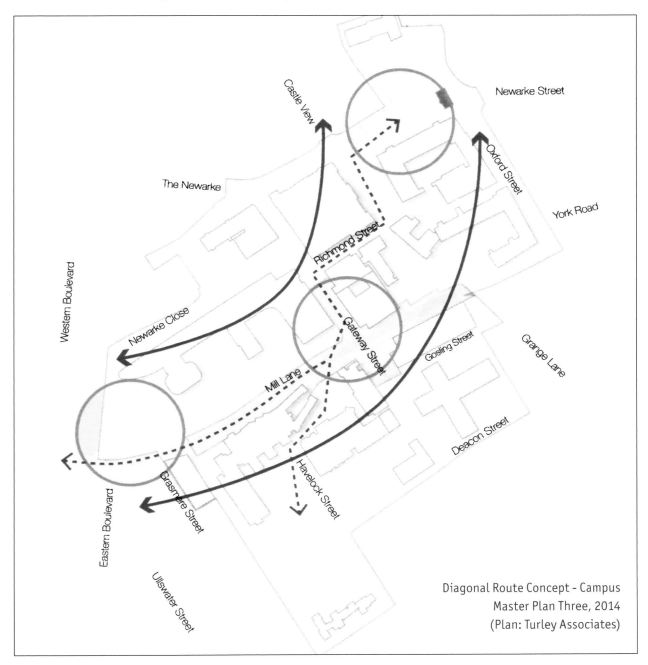

Diagonal Route Concept - Campus Master Plan Three, 2014 (Plan: Turley Associates)

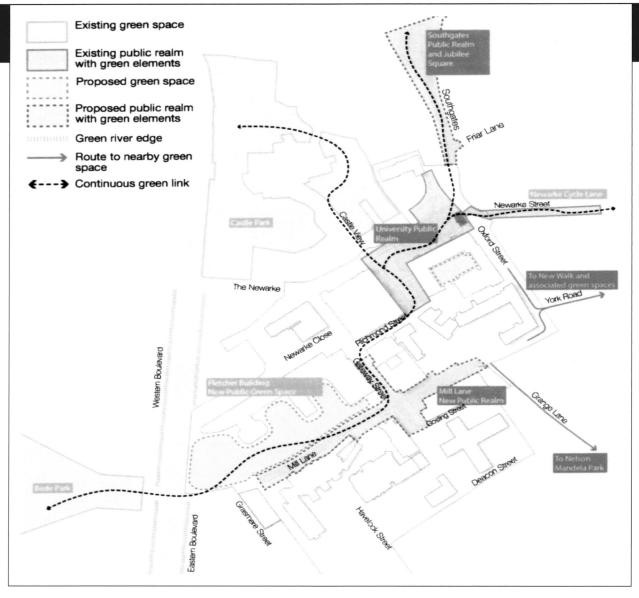

Legend:

- Existing green space
- Existing public realm with green elements
- Proposed green space
- Proposed public realm with green elements
- Green river edge
- Route to nearby green space
- Continuous green link

Southgates Public Realm and Jubilee Square

Newarke Cycle Lane

University Public Realm

To New Walk and associated green spaces

Castle Park

Fletcher Building New Public Green Space

Mill Lane New Public Realm

To Nelson Mandela Park

Beale Park

The Newarke

Castle View

Southgates

Friar Lane

Newarke Street

Oxford Street

York Road

Newarke Close

Richmond Street

Gateway Street

Grange Lane

Gosling Street

Deacon Street

Western Boulevard

Eastern Boulevard

Grasmere Street

Mill Lane

Havelock Street

New buildings completed on the university campus during the development period from 2002 include the Campus Centre (2003), the Performance Arts Centre for Excellence (2007), the Hugh Aston Building (2010), the De Montfort Surgery (2011), the Queen Elizabeth II Diamond Jubilee Leisure Centre (2012) and the Vijay Patel Building (2016). Major refurbishments include the Chancellor's House and the Philip Tasker Building (2010), Edith Murphy House (2011), the Venue (2015) and Leicester Castle (2016).

Green Network - Campus Master Plan Three, 2014 (Plan: Turley Associates)

Mill Lane - Campus Master Plan Three, 2014 (Plan: Turley Associates)

University of Leicester
Buildings on the Central Campus

(Original plan: University of Leicester)

Legend:
- Before 1950
- 1950s
- 1960s
- 1970s
- 1980s
- 1990s
- 2000s
- 2010s

Fielding Johnson Building

The original classical Fielding Johnson Building was built in phases as the Leicestershire and Rutland Lunatic Asylum. The main north-west frontage was designed in 1837 by William Parsons, the architect of the local Welford Road Leicester Prison and Mr Wallett, the superintendent of the Dorset County Asylum at Dorchester. Built in buff stock brick of predominantly two storeys, but with the centre and terminal pavilions emphasised by three storeys, the building is an appealing example of well-balanced Georgian architecture. The façade is articulated with a sandstone plinth and cills and originally a limestone cornice.

The red brick wings were added in 1842, and extended by Parsons and Dain in 1848-49. Further additions in 1858 were a third storey to the central sections of the two wings, together with a chapel and recreational hall behind the front entrance. Here, externally, a combination of Flemish bond white Mountsorrel bricks and Bangor slates was used. Other outbuildings were added towards the end of the nineteenth century. During the mid-nineteenth century, the building was surrounded only by open parkland and hand-cultivated land, with the 1849 cemetery on the city side of University Road, known firstly as Occupation Road, then in 1928 as Victoria Road. The adjacent Victoria Park opened in 1883.

The Leicestershire and Rutland Lunatic Asylum in 1849 (Photograph: University of Leicester Archive)

College Campus in the early 1950s
(Photograph: University of Leicester Archive)

Whilst the idea of a University College or University in Leicester was mooted as early as 1880, no resources were forthcoming at that time. However, the asylum building was vacated in 1907, when the County Asylum at Carlton Hayes was opened. The war intervened and the building was requisitioned as the 5th Northern General Hospital. During the war many additional temporary buildings were designed by Samuel Perkins Pick and built behind the main building to take in more war wounded, but after the war the complex again became vacant. It was secretly purchased in 1919, by Thomas Fielding Johnson, a local worsted manufacturer, who donated the buildings and six acres for a higher education college, whilst giving the remaining thirty one acres for the Boys and Girls Wyggeston Grammar Schools. The Leicester, Leicestershire and Rutland College opened to its first students in 1921, in the original building which was officially named after Thomas Fielding Johnson only in 1964.

Modifications to the Fielding Johnson Building continued. The major quadrangle was closed off in 1947-48 by Pick Everard Keay and Gimson and in 1952-54 Shirley Worthington built the first purpose-built library across the centre of the major quadrangle. This space now holds the Harry Peach Law Library.

Minor buildings were demolished for the Engineering Building and the south-east 1848 extension was removed to be replaced by the 1971 library. Thus the remaining Fielding Johnson Building consists of a single rectangular plan of

Rear entrance - 1953

Harry Peach Law Library

University Campus in 1968
(Photograph: University of Leicester Archive, printed from the Leicester Mercury)

the earliest construction divided centrally by the former chapel and recreational room into the two quadrangles, originally used for exercise by asylum residents, and the south-west wing of 1848, behind the new library. The medical superintendent's house of 1872 remains as College House. One of the two isolated extensions of 1895 and the stable block to the south-east, belong to the Wyggeston and Queen Elizabeth I College, the other extension adjacent to the Engineering Building is used by that Department.

The World War I nurses home in the foreground of the 1968 photograph was used as the women's hostel, then by Arts and Social Sciences staff until it was demolished after the Attenborough Building opened.

Since 1970, the lawn in front of the Fielding Johnson Building has featured major sculptures. Initially Henry Moore loaned his 'Draped Seated Woman', but this was removed a year later and replaced by his exquisite work, 'Oval with Points'. The University marked Henry Moore's act of generosity by awarding him an honorary degree. Unfortunately 'Oval with Points' was removed in 1987 by his estate after Henry Moore's death the previous year. Both 'Oval with Points' and 'Draped Seated Woman' (1958) are currently located in the Yorkshire Sculpture Park near Wakefield.

However, in 1990 the University was fortunate to acquire 'Souls' by Helaine Blumenfeld and this now is the focal point of the main lawn. The west courtyard has the 'Triangulated Form' sculpture (1960) by Robert Adams.

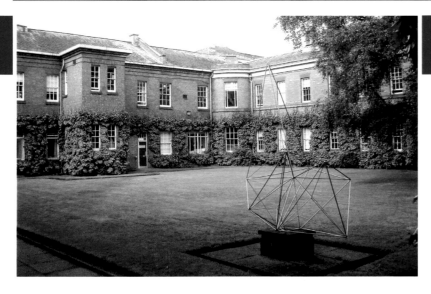

'Triangulated Form'
by Robert Adams, 1960

'Draped Seated Woman'
by Henry Moore, 1958
(Photograph: The University
of Leicester, Brian Burch)

'Oval with Points'
by Henry Moore, 1968-70
(Photograph: The University
of Leicester, Brian Burch)

'Souls' by Helaine Blumenfeld,
1990

North quadrangle

The 1965 Council Chamber

The Fielding Johnson Building now houses part of the College of Social Sciences, Arts & Humanities and University Professional Services, including the Office of the President and Vice-Chancellor. The original chapel of 1858, clearly articulated by its arched windows to the courtyards and raised roof-line was remodelled by Trevor Dannatt to be the University Council Room. However, the 1965 lowered ceiling has now been removed to expose the original early Victorian structure. The architects Shepheard Epstein Hunter also restored the tripartite stone windows to their original form. Within the Council Chamber is a Ceremonial Chair, designed by the College architect, Keay, made by Ernest Gimson's chief workman, Mr Waals, and presented to the College in 1923 by Mr and Mrs A.F. Cholerton. The chair is inlaid with ivory and carries the inscription 'UT VITAM HABEANT', 'so that they may have life' – the University's motto.

The remodelled Council Chamber

Ceremonial Chair, 1923

The walls of the Council Chamber carry portraits of the Chairmen of the College Council, College Principals, Chancellor and Vice-Chancellors of the University together with a number of pencil sketches of senior figures associated with the University.

The original site entrance was past the lodge, built in 1896, which is currently used by the University security staff.

The main façade of the Fielding Johnson Building is listed Grade II. Thomas Fielding Johnson born in 1828, was awarded the Honorary Freedom of the City of Leicester in 1919 and died in 1921.

The Lodge – side entrance

The Lodge, 1896

Chaplaincy

The interdenominational Chaplaincy occupies the lodge to the Welford Road Cemetery in University Road. Originally the Welford Road cemetery had a large Church of England Chapel and a Non-conformist Chapel, but these were demolished in 1958 when they became obsolete, due to the opening of the Gilroes Crematorium to the north of the City. The lodge was built in c.1850, when Flint, the architect to the Corporation, noted that the cost of the lodge and cottages would be £900. The Chaplaincy Centre opened to all students of the University in the early 1990s under the name 'The Gatehouse'.

Leicester Wyvern

Octagon - 1990

The 1990 octagonal addition by the Douglas Smith Stimson Partnership has an interesting exposed steel-supported roof structure incorporating roof light glazing.

College House

The College House was built as part of the original asylum in 1872 as the residence for the Medical Superintendent. It was designed by Dain and Smith architects and was connected to the main building by a covered way. It became the home of the first Principal of the College, Dr Rattray and subsequently for the second Principal, Frederick L. Attenborough from 1931 to 1951. Frederick Attenborough and his wife (a Justice of the Peace), lived in College House during the adolescent years of their three sons; Richard, David and John.

Internally the building has been modified for educational use, although the main staircase remains virtually intact. The building since 1951 has supported many functions, and currently houses the Department of Informatics.

Astley Clarke Building

The Astley Clarke Building, completed in 1951, was the first new building on the campus since the College opened in 1921. It was designed by Pick Everard Keay and Gimson to a layout previously developed by T. Shirley Worthington of Thomas Worthington & Sons, Manchester. It was designed to accommodate the Botany and Zoology Departments and was built by Chitham of Leicester.

The building's neo-Georgian style harmonises with the Fielding Johnson Building, through its local pale buff brickwork, appropriate fenestration and parapet to the short front elevation. The brickwork is articulated by a stone cornice, decorative stonework to the entrances and well detailed rainwater goods. To the other elevations, the Swithland slated Mansard roof creates a modest

scale to the three storey building (plus basement), which won a bronze medal design award from the Royal Institute of British Architects. The main entrance foyer and staircase are clad in travertine marble.

This building, together with the 1995 Ken Edwards building, effectively frames the original Fielding Johnson Building to form a partial enclosure of the front lawn focusing on the

sculptural centrepiece. The Astley Clarke building is named after Dr Astley V. Clarke, who in 1912, as President of the Literary and Philosophical Society, strongly supported the establishment of a university or university college in Leicester. Dr Astley Clarke became Chairman of the College Council from 1939 to 1945. The Astley Clarke Building now houses part of the School of Business.

Percy Gee Building

The Percy Gee Building, completed in 1958, was the second new building on the campus designed by T. Shirley Worthington of Thomas Worthington & Sons, Manchester, as part of his campus plan. It was also his last building on the main campus as his services were no longer required once Leslie Martin had been appointed as the campus plan architect. The Students' Union building has a large hall (Queen's Hall) for concerts, lectures etc. and provides social facilities for the student population including bars, shop, refectory, offices and common rooms. It was built by F. Perks & Sons Ltd. of Long Eaton in Derbyshire.

The building is described by Pevsner as being 'pale and anaemic', but this is harsh criticism, as the brickwork is of a distinctly warmer colour than that of its predecessor, the Astley Clarke Building; it also exhibits a copper roof. Stylistically it is a calculated move away from that previous neo-Georgian construction to a typical academic building of the fifties, incorporating standard metal framed-windows. Indeed it was this very 'normality' that led to Worthington's replacement as university architect by Leslie Martin. The building had interior level changes which made circulation difficult; however, externally it has some interesting details including gryphon crests on the rainwater pipes and the University Coat of Arms over the doorway.

(Photograph:
University of Leicester)

University Coat of Arms

The Percy Gee Building is named after Mr Harry Percy Gee, CBE, LLD, JP, who succeeded Dr Astley Clarke as Chairman of the College Council from 1945 to University status in 1957, when he became Pro-Chancellor until 1962. Percy Gee, a prominent civic figure, had strongly supported the development of the University College. He was High Sheriff of Leicestershire in 1942 and was awarded the Freedom of the City of Leicester in 1950. He, as one of the foremost founding fathers of the University College was highly respected both by the University and the City.

The front foyer of the Percy Gee building is finished in travertine marble, similar to the Astley Clarke building, and has the plaque unveiled by Her Majesty The Queen and HRH Prince Philip, Duke of Edinburgh at the official opening of the building on 9 May 1958.

Original University Road frontage

Commemorative plaque

THE PERCY GEE BUILDING
THIS BUILDING WAS OPENED BY
HER MAJESTY QUEEN ELIZABETH II
ON THE OCCASION OF HER VISIT TO
THE UNIVERSITY OF LEICESTER
WITH
HRH PRINCE PHILIP DUKE OF EDINBURGH
9 MAY 1958

Rainwater head detail

A major £17m refurbishment and enhancement designed by Shepheard Epstein Hunter and constructed by Morgan Sindall plc was officially opened in March 2011 by Aaron Porter, President of the National Union of Students and a University of Leicester graduate who had led the Students' Union Executive. The project has created a central atrium supported by curved glulam beams. The building provides catering, social, retail, educational and live venue facilities extending

Official Opening of the Percy Gee Building by Her Majesty The Queen and HRH Prince Philip Duke of Edinburgh, 1958 (Photograph: 'The University of Leicester', Brian Burch, from the Leicester Mercury)

Terrace

Atrium

to a new façade and terrace towards University Road. The work included the provision of a woodchip biomass boiler, a rainwater harvesting system to provide flushing water for toilets, also enhanced natural ventilation and lighting to reduce energy consumption. Mechanical air conditioning is only required for the nightclub when activated by the carbon dioxide sensors. Key to disabled access was the elimination of the many changes in level within the original building. At the official opening of the building the sculpture 'Touching Pair' by Deirdre Hubbard FRBS which stands in the circulation area was also unveiled.

The project has gained several awards including the Leicester Civic Society Architecture Award for New Build (2010) and the Best Large Commercial Development in the Local Authority Building Control Regional Awards (2011).

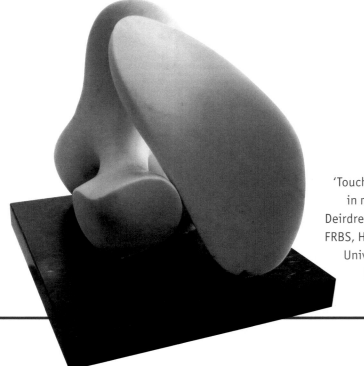

'Touching Pair' in marble by Deirdre Hubbard FRBS, Hon D.Litt University of Leicester

George Porter and Archaeology & Ancient History Buildings

The George Porter Chemistry and the Archaeology & Ancient History Buildings, (originally Chemistry Teaching 1960 and Chemistry Research 1961 respectively), were the first buildings constructed to the 1957 Leslie Martin campus plan to the east of Mayor's Walk, and as such were a stylistic break from the Astley Clarke and Percy Gee buildings designed by Worthington. The two buildings were designed by the Architects Co-Partnership, a practice founded in 1939 which in the 60s was focussed on the public and institutional sectors including educational buildings. The enlarged practice currently operates from Hertfordshire. Both buildings were constructed by Wilson Lovatt & Sons Ltd. of Wolverhampton.

The buildings are located according to the Leslie Martin plan, which specified the positions and massing to create the various terraces on the sloping site. The courtyards are enhanced by a combination of hard and soft landscaping. Both buildings

Archaeology & Ancient History Building

George Porter Chemistry Building

have a strong horizontal emphasis, but the materials are treated differently. The Archaeology & Ancient History Building uses yellow brickwork to link in with the other Leslie Martin science buildings, and this is banded with the fenestration set in black exposed aggregate concrete panels. The George Porter Building further emphasises the horizontality with sandwiched black and blue spandrels alternating with the glazing to the three floors above the central courtyard level. The featured black finish of ceramic mosaic is combined with areas of white mosaic particularly to the courtyard elevation. The lower level, associated with the sloping site, is built in the yellow brickwork, frequently used in this area of the campus. These two science buildings form part of the sensitively designed intimate part of the Leslie Martin campus. The Archaeology and Ancient History Building was accommodation for chemistry research until a refurbishment in 2003.

King Richard III (1483 – 1485)
St Martin's Cathedral, Leicester

'Life' by Percy Brown,
1976

The Department of Chemistry teaching building was named in 2001 after George Porter, Baron Porter of Luddenham, OM FRS and winner of the Nobel Prize for Chemistry in 1967. George Porter was knighted in 1972, made a life peer in 1990 and was Chancellor of the University from 1984 to 1995.

The University of Leicester Archaeological Services Unit based in the School of Archaeology and Ancient History, together with the Richard III Society, were responsible for the remarkable discovery of King Richard III's skeleton under the remains of Leicester's Grey Friars Franciscan friary. DNA analysis, originally developed in the University of Leicester, was able to confirm that the skeleton discovered was that of Richard III, and it was

finally reinterred in a prominent location within the Cathedral of St Martin, Leicester.

The open space between the two science buildings is enhanced with a charming sculpture by Percy Brown named 'Life', which has a hint of Barbara Hepworth influence.

George Porter Chemistry Building
(Photograph: University of Leicester)

Physics Building

The Physics Building, designed by Leslie Martin and Colin St John Wilson, was built in 1961 by Wilson Lovatt & Sons Ltd. Colin St John (Sandy) Wilson's early experience as architect was with the London County Council architects department, and when Leslie Martin moved from there to take up his professorial post at Cambridge, Sandy Wilson also moved with him to be a lecturer in the Cambridge School of Architecture. Leslie Martin and Sandy Wilson then worked on several projects together in Oxford, Cambridge and Leicester.

The concrete frame Physics Building is clad in yellow brickwork, sympathetic to many of the other adjacent Leslie Martin buildings. The low impact, two-storey elevations are characterised by the continuous clerestory glazing on both floors, capped to the upper storey with black exposed aggregate concrete cladding. The façade is only articulated by the recessed stepped entrance. The interior staircases and the spine corridors have exposed yellow brickwork with wood block floors. An additional storey for office accommodation was added in 1983 by Castle Park Hook Whitehead Stanway, the London practice who had previously designed the 1974 Library and Villiers Hall in Oadby.

The Physics Building currently provides teaching and office accommodation for the Department of Physics and Astronomy within the College of Science and Engineering.

Rattray Lecture Theatre

The Rattray Lecture Theatre was designed by Leslie Martin and Colin St John Wilson and built in 1962 by Wilson Lovatt & Sons Ltd.

The cuboid building is clad in yellow brickwork, in common with the adjacent Leslie Martin buildings. The two-storey building is entered from the main terrace but extends below using the slope of the site to advantage. The ground floor is naturally lit by a clerestory. An appropriate addition was the glazed lift to improve disabled access. The lower level accommodates a café.

Astronomical Clock

Glazed Lift

(Photograph: University of Leicester)

A key feature is the astronomical clock on the front façade. It was designed by Dr Allan Mills and Ralph Jefferson of the Department of Geology and unveiled in July 1989 by the astronomer Dr Heather Couper CBE, a graduate of the University and the first woman President of the British Astronomical Association who is now a well known international writer and broadcaster on astronomy and space.

The building is named after Dr R.F. Rattray MA PhD, the first Principal of the University College from 1921 to 1931.

Engineering Building

The most famous and internationally recognised building on the university campus is undoubtedly the Engineering Building (1959-63) designed by James Stirling and James Gowan and built by Wilson Lovatt & Sons Ltd. The architects were appointed in 1959, on the suggestion of Leslie Martin who had been working on the master plan for the campus since 1957 when the university became independent. The site had been rather left out of the master plan, and Leslie Martin considered that Stirling & Gowan would produce something unique. The brief was largely a schedule of accommodation, with a requirement for an 80ft (24m) tower to produce the requisite head of water for the engineering activities, and no exposed concrete surfaces as the 'brutalism' of boardmarked concrete was becoming unfashionable.

The design progressed through a number of iterations, but ultimately produced a final scheme which on completion produced extremes of reaction. However, it was soon realised that Stirling & Gowan had designed for the university a spectacular building, which today is recognised as a landmark in twentieth century architecture by one of the greatest post-war British architects, James Stirling. The building continues to attract world-wide interest, particularly from students of architecture. The building was featured in a set of four commemorative stamps issued in 1971, which illustrated high quality new university architecture.

The building massing is characterised by the two towers, one tall and translucent, the other banded to indicate the floor levels, each rising from their cantilevered lecture theatres, with the taller tower defining the main entrance.

Commemorative Stamp, 1971

The lower four-storey tower of laboratories has bands of projecting windows to enhance the cross-ventilation, thus economising on air-conditioning. The towers are clad in red Accrington brick with matching Dutch red tiles over any other areas of in-situ concrete work including soffits. Where tiles were required, the concrete was cast against profiled rubber sheeting, producing a good key for subsequent fixing of the dovetail-backed tiles. Patent glazing was used for the towers, despite James Stirling pressing for the elegance of plate glass, but this proved too expensive within the constraints of the University Grants Committee budget.

The teaching workshops, covering over two thirds of the site, are defined by their prismatic roof set at 45° to the walls, creating a crystalline form which glows after dark over the storey-high brick plinth. The rationale was the requirement for true north light within clear span, flexible workshops. The lighting control was achieved with a sandwich of fibreglass between two sheets of glass, to which an additional blocking aluminium layer was added on the south facing elements. This composite double-glazing was set within the aluminium patent glazing system.

The partially cantilevered lecture theatres are stabilised by the massive towers above. The steep rake permits good visibility to the lecturer and demonstration bench. The faceted glass enclosure for the spiral stair from the podium to the main lecture theatre admits latecomers without disturbance.

Entrance Foyer

Since the building was completed in 1963, it had in 1985, a major refurbishment to the tower glazing, which now exhibits visually heavier sections than the original aluminium curtain walling system, but is thermally more efficient. The workshops, which suffered from some overheating during summer periods and rainwater penetration, have recently been refurbished to rectify these issues. Details of the glazing system were agreed between English Heritage, the

Roof replacement mock-up

History Faculty Building at Cambridge University – James Stirling, 1966

Twentieth Century Society, the local authority and Arup engineers, within the constraints of a listed building. A double-layer outer glass pane with a fibre interlayer, fabricated within a double-glazed system, preserves the characteristic appearance of the original roof by day and by night. A mock-up of the approved replacement roof system is displayed on the campus.

Despite the initial controversy it caused and necessary subsequent maintenance, the Engineering Building remains pivotal in post-modern architecture; it established James Stirling's reputation, and having broken the mould of the Leslie Martin restrained campus design, opened the way for the subsequent Denys Lasdun (Charles Wilson Building) and Arup Associates (Attenborough Building) towers.

The building received the prestigious R.S. Reynolds Memorial Award in 1965 from The American Institute of Architects, for 'honoring a significant work of architecture in which aluminium has been an important contributory factor'. It was listed Grade II* in 1993 by the Department of National Heritage. In 2008 the Engineering Building was named by 'The Telegraph' as one of Britain's top fifty most inspiring buildings. The building is home for the Department of Engineering within the College of Science and Engineering.

The University of Leicester Engineering Building blazed the trail towards Stirling's equally renowned 1968 University of Cambridge, History Faculty Building, built in similar materials - hard red brick with an aluminium glazing system.

Bennett Building

The Bennett Building, designed by Leslie Martin and Colin St John Wilson in association with Castle & Park, was built in 1965 by Johnson & Bailey Ltd. The concrete frame building is clad in yellow brickwork, in common with many of the other adjacent Leslie Martin buildings. It has direct aesthetic continuity with the Physics Building, which had been completed just fours years previously, by using similar yellow brickwork and grey-painted concrete cladding, but the Bennett Building differs, having continuous bands of brickwork and windows. The three-storey building is entered at first floor level from the hard landscaped courtyard which forms a bridge over the subway connection. The Bennett Building closes off the end of the campus towards the Lutyens War Memorial, creating the collegiate enclosure designed by Leslie Martin.

The Bennett Building entered construction history, because of an unfortunate incident on the night of 12 June 1973, when part of the roof collapsed. A few minutes before the incident a student and two cleaners noticed cracks appearing, and fortunately they left the building before the collapse occurred, so no-one was injured. Within a short period, two other similar building failures occurred at schools in Camden and Stepney. Initially it was thought that poor workmanship was the cause of these failures. If so, why had these buildings lasted for nearly a decade before failure? Soon, detailed analysis made it clear that the High Alumina Cement (calcium aluminate cement) concrete had deteriorated over a period of eight years by a process of conversion, in which changes in crystal structure accelerated by warmth and humidity had caused serious loss of strength, increased porosity and the risk of further chemical attack. The consequence of these building failures was a total ban on the use of calcium aluminate cement concrete for all subsequent structural work; a ban still in force today within many European countries.

The Bennett Building was completely closed after the incident, and an additional stainless steel frame inserted, to relieve the loading on the calcium aluminate cement concrete structure. Subsequently some additional strengthening was also added to the Physics Building without its closure but causing considerable disruption to its day-to-day operation. The Bennett Link runs underneath the hard landscaped quadrangle.

The building currently provides teaching and office accommodation for the Departments of Geography and Geology.

Bennett Entrance Foyer

Bennett Building Sundials

The building is named after Dr Frederick W. Bennett, a long-standing benefactor of the University College, who together with Dr Astley Clarke in 1918 opened a fund for the endowment of a University College for Leicester.

Adrian Building

The Adrian Building designed by Courtauld Technical Services Ltd. Coventry, who then became W.F. Johnson & Partners of Leamington Spa, was built in 1966 by Johnson & Co. Ltd. Leicester. The building is a long concrete frame structure clad in white tiles. The building was originally planned to be smaller but against the advice of Sir Leslie Martin, the university architect at that time, the plans were enlarged to reflect the expectations of the Robbins report on university expansion and specifically the University of Leicester's own increased target figures. The building does however effectively close off the original rectangle associated with the Sir Leslie Martin campus plan.

The white tile-clad construction was typical of many university buildings of that era. In particular, the new University of Warwick was opening near Coventry. The University of Warwick had started on a small scale in 1965, but in 1966 was building the main campus including the library block. Their building soon ran into difficulties with white tiles falling off the building façade. This was eventually resolved with plastic over-cladding. Fortunately,

Mosaic canopy feature

the University of Leicester Adrian Building, although also clad in white tiles, did not suffer the same problem.

To the University Road side of the Adrian Building is a coloured mosaic clad 'ship's prow complete with copper mast'. This decorative feature, acting as a canopy, is however somewhat lost against the later addition of the steel bridge over the street linking to the Maurice Shock Medical Sciences Building.

The white tile Adrian building is a total break from the more sophisticated yellow brick and black concrete banding associated with the earlier Leslie Martin buildings within the science zone of the campus. The building of four storeys arguably uses the considerable slope on the site to retain a roof line compatible with the other science buildings, but its height creates a massing of a different scale to the adjacent earlier blocks.

The building has teaching and office accommodation for Molecular and Medical Sciences. The building is named after Lord Adrian, President of the College from 1955 to 1957, who then became first Chancellor of the University until his retirement in 1971. Lord Adrian officially opened the building in 1968.

Bridge over University Road

Charles Wilson Building

The Charles Wilson Building (1962-67) was designed by Denys Lasdun and Partners, whose work also includes the Royal National Theatre and the Grade I listed Royal College of Physicians together other prominent university buildings at Cambridge, London and Norwich. The contractor was Johnson and Bailey Ltd. of Cambridge.

The building is located on the former bowling green; a site that had been provisionally allocated in Leslie Martin campus planning to the Council and Senate Building. The typical Lasdun style emphasises the horizontality of the broader six storey block with concrete and glass banding and contrasts this to the verticality of the tower. However, the horizontality is realised with more sensitivity than is seen in the heavier Royal National Theatre in London.

It was during this period of the early 60s, that the University was reviewing upwards its student target numbers, and this was subsequently reinforced by the Robbins Report on increased university access which was accepted in principle by the Government in 1963, who then promised to resource the necessary building expansion programme. As a consequence, the additional top five floors were added to the original design for the Charles Wilson building, giving the effect of blocks on blocks, a characteristic of Denys Lasdun's architecture seen particularly in the 'ziggurat' accommodation of the University of East Anglia and the Royal College of Physicians in London.

The building, of exposed fairfaced concrete construction, has generally matured well into its site, and still offers staff and students many of the original functions, including the Student Services Centre, a large sports facility and several self-service and restaurant outlets with open views towards Victoria Park. The entrance features buff brickwork and this is carried through into the entrance foyer walls, floor and stairs. Some pattern staining and spalling of the concrete finish has affected the exterior.

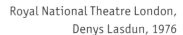

Royal National Theatre London,
Denys Lasdun, 1976

University Clock,
2003

'Relief Construction: After-Images'
by Colin Jones, 1983

The University Clock is located adjacent to the main entrance directly on the buff brickwork façade. It commemorates Arthur Humphreys, the College and University's first Professor of English. It was unveiled in September 2003.

To the rear of the building is the artwork 'Relief Construction: After-Images' 1983 by Colin Jones.

The building is named after Charles H. Wilson who was the Principal of the College from 1951 to 1957 and the University's first Vice-Chancellor from 1957 to 1961. It was Charles Wilson who made the first public announcement in 1954, that the College would petition The Queen for independent status in 1956. The building was granted a Civic Trust Award in 1969.

Attenborough Building

The Attenborough Building was designed by Sir Philip Dowson of Arup Associates, with Ove Arup as consulting engineers and completed by John Laing Construction Ltd. in 1970 on the site of the former nurses' hostel. Originally the Arts and Social Sciences tower was conceived as the first of three tower blocks within the campus development plan because of restricted space, but the additional two towers never materialised and gradually attitudes towards high rise buildings changed, so subsequent university development was of low and medium rise. The three towers, trefoil in plan form to retain visual slenderness, were to be connected at low level.

The 48m, eighteen storey tower provides three leaves of tutorial and staff room accommodation serviced with a central lift and paternoster. This is now the only remaining paternoster in Leicester since the removal of the paternoster from the Vijay Patel Building at De Montfort University. The main teaching spaces, including two lecture theatres and film theatre (formerly a performance theatre), are linked to the four storey seminar building which is partly below ground level. The underground lecture theatres form a raised brick-paved piazza to the front entrance of the building leading towards the library.

The building on pile foundations consists of an in-situ concrete frame, and the majority of the tower is clad in precast concrete panels with aluminium-framed glazing. The base of the tower in yellow-buff brick reflects the construction of the earlier campus buildings. The low rise teaching block is constructed in exposed concrete with some brickwork infill, to empathise with the form and materials of the adjacent Charles Wilson Building by Denys Lasdun.

The Attenborough Building has been nicknamed 'the cheese grater' by students because of its characteristic appearance, with the outward slanting windows designed to create draft-free ventilation through their soffits. A subsequent refurbishment has removed the soffit ventilation and replaced the glazing with blue-tinted solar-control glass. The opening triangular sidelights are retained. The original glazing feature was criticised by Nikolaus Pevsner in 1984 as being 'prickly' and 'more successful inside than out'. The building has been refurbished to comply with the Disability Discrimination Act with respect to vertical circulation, and also to clean the external concrete finish, which had been affected by pattern staining from the rainwater run-off.

Refurbished window and campus view

'Eye of Time' by Allan Mills, 2007

The building is named after Mr F.L. Attenborough, Principal of the University College from 1932 to 1951. It was opened by his youngest son, John in 1970 as Frederick Attenborough was infirm at that time. On the same day both Richard and David Attenborough received honorary degrees of the University. Richard and David Attenborough were each given the Freedom of the City of Leicester in November 1989. The University conferred Richard and David Attenborough as Distinguished Honorary Fellows of the University in July 2006.

The building offers good views of the city and received a Civic Trust Commendation in 1972. Its location is enhanced by the sculpture 'Eye of Time' by Allan Mills which was sculpted by Fairhaven of Anglesey Abbey Ltd. and unveiled by Richard Attenborough in June 2007. The tower houses part of the College of Social Sciences, Arts and Humanities.

Maurice Shock Building

The Maurice Shock Building designed by W.F. Johnson & Partners of Leamington Spa, was completed in 1977 by Taylor Woodrow Construction (Midlands) Ltd.

The six-storey concrete frame building is clad with exposed aggregate ribbed concrete panels, which show some weathering patterns. The entrances are emphasised by the glazed stairwells set within the deep purple/grey brickwork which is carried through to the roof storey and the hard landscaping to the street frontage. The glazing alternates along the façade with black glazed-over panels. The front of the building is linked across University Road to the Adrian Building. In addition the rear of the building is linked by bridges to the two newer buildings,

Main entrance to University Road

the Hodgkin Building and the Henry Wellcome Building respectively.

The Maurice Shock Building was officially opened by Sir Cyril Clarke, KBE MD FRCP FRS son of Dr Astley V. Clarke in 1977. In 1994 the building was renamed the Maurice Shock Medical Sciences Building, after Sir Maurice Shock MA LLD who was Vice-Chancellor of the University from 1977 to 1987. The building provides laboratory and teaching accommodation for the Medical School within the College of Medicine, Biological Sciences and Psychology.

The associated Clinical Sciences Building, located at the Leicester Royal Infirmary, was designed by Pick Everard Keay and Gimson and completed in 1978 by R.G. Carter (Kings Lynn) Ltd. It was

(Photograph: University of Leicester)

named after Professor Sir Robert Kilpatrick who was the second Dean of Medicine of the University from 1975 to 1989. The building provides teaching accommodation for students undertaking clinical training, together with staff offices and research facilities. Sir Robert Kilpatrick, Baron Kilpatrick of Kincraig CBE, was invested with a life peerage in 1996.

Panel detail

Bridge to Hodgkin building

Computer Centre and Materials Centre

The Computer Centre and Materials Centre building was designed by Castle Park Hook Whitehead Stanway (formerly Castle Park Dean Hook in the 1970s) and completed in 1985 by Ford & Weston Ltd. It had been intended to build a centre for the University's mainframe computer as early as 1978; however, national restrictions on university funding delayed the start until 1984. By that time the Wolfson Foundation had agreed to fund accommodation for the new Biotechnology Unit to support the university's initiative in biotechnology, so the new building was finally designed to house the University Computer Centre and the Biocentre for biochemistry. The building continues to accommodate the university Computer Centre but with the Department of Chemistry Materials Centre to the rear.

The building of steel construction on round concrete columns, features orange/red banding, quoins and cills to the buff yellow brickwork associated with much of the campus. The building features deep shading eaves under the plastic coated sheet steel roof, and cultivates a low snug aesthetic on the site, adjacent to the entrance up Mayor's Walk.

Polychromatic brickwork detail

Informatics Building

Banded brickwork detail

The Informatics Building was designed by Castle Park Hook Stanway and built in 1990 by J.C. Kellet & Son Ltd. of Leicester. It occupies a prime site within the University Campus.

The two-storey building of steel frame construction is clad in polychromatic brickwork which was popular in commercial and academic buildings at that period. The red and buff banding is highlighted by single courses of blue brick. The brickwork is articulated to emphasise the steel structure which emerges to the first floor clerestory. The eaves offer some shading to the upper storey glazing.

The building accommodates the Department of Informatics lecture, seminar and teaching rooms together with staff offices. The building was officially opened in 1991 by Lord Lawson, Chancellor of the Exchequer from 1983 to 1989.

Hodgkin Building

The Hodgkin Building on Lancaster Road was designed by Castle Park Hook and Partners and completed in 1993. The six-storey building is characterised by its polychromatic and banded brickwork. The predominantly deep purple creates a strong base from which the light buff top storeys rise. The two sections are linked by banding of the alternate colour. The deep eaves roof in sheet metal gives some shading to the upper storeys and partially obscures the servicing systems. The building is entered through a semi-circular canopy.

The Hodgkin Building is linked by an elevated walkway to the Maurice Shock Medical Sciences Building.

The Hodgkin Building which houses the Medical Research Council's Toxicology Unit is named after Professor Sir Alan Hodgkin, Chancellor of the University between 1971 and 1984. Sir Alan Hodgkin had a notable career winning the Nobel Prize in 1963, also being awarded a knighthood in 1961 and the Order of Merit in 1963. He was President of the Royal Society from 1970 to 1975 and Master of Trinity College

(Photograph: University of Leicester)

Cambridge from 1978 to 1984. The Hodgkin building was officially opened by Rt Hon William Waldegrave, Chancellor of the Duchy of Lancaster, Minister for Science, in 1993.

Banded brickwork detail

Lancaster Road elevation and bridge to the Maurice Shock Medical Sciences Building

Ken Edwards Building

The Ken Edwards Building was designed by the Park Leech Partnership in association with Hook Whitehead Stanway, who had previously designed the first phase of the library in 1974 and subsequently the Computer Centre and the Informatics Building. The building with three floors above main site level and with two basement levels using the natural slope of the site, was built to mirror the earlier Astley Clarke Building, which it accurately reflects. In this respect the building with its buff brickwork, fenestration, stone string courses and cornice is very effective. However, the central section of the building is not a true Mansard roof and is built with modern slates rather than the naturally variable traditional slates of the Astley Clarke Building. The basement floors in buff/cream render act as an appropriate plinth for the upper three stories keeping the required visual scale and massing.

The Ken Edwards Building provides accommodation for the School of Business. The building has three large lecture rooms in addition

to modern teaching and research facilities.

The building is named after Dr Kenneth Edwards who was the University Vice-Chancellor from 1987 to 1999. The building was officially opened by Sir Michael Atiyah OM FRS, Chancellor of the University, in September 1995.

(Photograph: University of Leicester)

Attenborough Arts Centre

The Attenborough Arts Centre founded by the late Lord Richard Attenborough is located on Lancaster Road. The original building was designed by Bennetts Associates and completed in 1996. The building is constructed in load bearing brickwork, with a structural glass atrium, timber cladding and pale-grey metal window frames. The building encapsulates Richard Attenborough's vision to include everyone in art, culture and learning regardless of their abilities and background. The successful design was the result of an architectural competition and offers a visual and performing arts centre, with workshops and studios, incorporating activities for families and children. The design with well-lit interior spaces had been appropriately described as 'discrete and politely modern' when it was shortlisted for the 1998 Stirling Prize. The building was officially opened in 1997, by Diana, Princess of Wales and was the RIBA's 'Building of the Year' for the Education and Health sectors.

The centre was increased in size by the addition of a £1.5m extension designed by GSS Architecture and constructed by Stepnell Ltd. The New Galleries Wing incorporates three exhibition spaces, a creative space and an outdoor sculpture court. It was officially opened by Sir David Attenborough in January 2016.

The New Galleries Wing

Interior details

The official opening of the New Galleries Wing by Sir David Attenborough with the President and Vice-Chancellor Professor Paul Boyle

Gallery

(Photograph: David Wilson Clarke & University of Leicester)

Michael Atiyah Building

The Michael Atiyah Building was built in two phases which were opened in 1998 and 2002 respectively. The first phase was designed by the Park Leech Partnership and the second phase, towards the Engineering Building, was designed by Hook Whitehead Stanway. The first wing houses the Space Research Centre and the newer wing accommodates the Centre for Mathematical Modelling. The Michael Atiyah Building also accommodates the National Centre for Earth Observation.

The three-storey frame building is finished in proprietary beige reinforced thermosetting plastic rainscreen cladding, with grey painted exposed steelwork to the fire escapes. Shading devices over the windows reduce the risk of excessive solar gain and overheating. The east elevation overlooks the playing fields of the adjacent Wyggeston and Queen Elizabeth I College and is linked to the main campus by a pathway and vehicle access.

The Michael Aityah Building for the Departments of Physics & Astronomy, Engineering and Mathematics is named after Sir Michael Atiyah, Chancellor of the University between 1995 and 2005. The Space Research Centre was officially opened by John Battle, Minister of State for Science Engineering and Industry in April 1998. The exterior of the building is enhanced by a garden designed by a group led by Professor John Holloway, in which stands a bust of Sir Isaac Newton holding a sundial. The bronze sculpture is by Vanessa Stollery and the sundial by the astronomer, Dr John Davis.

'Sir Isaac Newton' by Vanessa Stollery and Dr John Davis

In 2011, a separate £1m Michael Atiyah Building annex, was officially opened by David Willetts, Minister for Universities and Science. Created under a design and build scheme by Premier Interlink and built by Morgan Sindall, the building was constructed within six months to October 2010.

Michael Atiyah Building Annex

Danielle Brown Sports Centre

The University acquired the former Nuffield Health Fitness and Wellbeing centre in April 2012. It was designed by Hooper Architects, built by Pillikaan and originally opened in 1998 as the Cannons Health Club on land that was part of the Wyggeston & Queen Elizabeth I College sports field. The complex offers a wide range of sport and health facilities including a swimming pool, sauna, sports hall and gymnasium. It complements the new sports and fitness centre on the Oadby campus, giving equivalent facilities for staff and students based on the central campus of the university. The centre is named after Danielle Brown MBE, a law graduate, who is a world-leading archer and gold medal winner in both Paralympic and able-bodied competition. The building was formally named and opened by Lord Grocott, Chancellor of the University of Leicester in September 2013.

20m swimming pool

Fitness centre

Sports hall

Henry Wellcome Building

The Henry Wellcome Building on Lancaster Road was designed by The Fairhursts Design Group, built by Norwest Holst and completed in 2004. The building accommodates biochemistry and psychology within the College of Medicine, Biological Sciences and Psychology, also the Frank and Katherine May Lecture Theatre named after Frank May MBE, a benefactor of the university.

The building is of concrete frame construction, clad in a combination of white plastic-coated metal panels, glass and featuring the aesthetic warmth of orange drag-face textured brickwork. Movement joints in the brickwork are disguised by horizontal bands of smooth recessed brickwork, which subtly break up the otherwise

(Photograph:
University of Leicester)

Building details

large brick façade with its punched windows. One part of the building, specifically for a powerful NMR (nuclear magnetic resonance) scanner requires the local absence of magnetic materials, so this area is constructed in fibre-reinforced concrete and non-magnetic reinforced brickwork under a timber roof. The ground floor of the building features a curved space, partly glazed to the south-facing offices and with curved brickwork to the north and west.

The six-storey building accommodates laboratory, research and teaching facilities, together with a coffee area. Offices, write-up spaces and meeting rooms are located with open south facing views. Laboratories are separated from offices by full height glass walls to permit daylight penetration and to facilitate the safe supervision of activities. A service corridor on the north side separates the laboratories from other office accommodation. The building is linked by an elevated walkway to the adjacent Maurice Shock Building.

The building has an attractive entrance foyer, leading to the Frank and Katherine May Lecture Theatre. The foyer is enhanced by several works of art including a painting by John Lancaster of the Faculty of Arts, Design and Humanities, De Montfort University. The dramatic main stairwell is centred by the spectacular 'Atomica' sculpture of 2005 by John Sydney Carter, FRBS.

The Henry Wellcome Building is named after Sir Henry Wellcome who in 1880 established the pharmaceutical company Burroughs Wellcome. A great philanthropist, Wellcome, upon his death in 1936, bequeathed the company shares to the Wellcome Trust who was charged with spending the income according to his wishes. Although the Wellcome Trust has a broad remit, the focus is on biomedical research to improve human and animal health. The building was officially opened by Dr Mark Walport, Director of the Wellcome Trust in 2006.

'Atomica' by John Sydney Carter
FRBS, 2005

'Vortex' by John Sydney Carter
FRBS, 2006

Bridge to the Maurice Shock building

Entrance foyer

Externally, in the courtyard between the Henry Wellcome and Hodgkin Buildings is the 'Vortex' sculpture by John Sydney Carter FRBS, which was donated by Hermes Real Estate in 2006.

David Wilson Library

Although the new university library was opened in April 2008, the history of the library dates back to the earliest period of the college. The library commenced with generous donations of personal book collections, including particularly a range of Topographical Books of England from a local businessman Thomas Hatton in 1920, and this was followed by many other significant bequests. The embryonic library was temporarily housed in the 'Pillar Room' of the Fielding Johnson Building for the first intake of students in 1921. The pillars were two wood Corinthian columns from a recently demolished 'Old Permanent Library' in the city. Soon, however, the library moved to a more appropriate location designed by William Keay, the college architect, and opened in 1923 by the newly appointed Visitor, Lord Haldene, on the first floor to the front of the building. The library then had six double-sided sets of oak book shelves, and six of the former cells set up as reading rooms. Incidentally, an annual prize is given in memory of William Keay to a worthy student of architecture at De Montfort University. The designed space too soon became insufficient and by 1933 the book collections were spread around four locations in the building. Further modifications to the building quickly proved inadequate and in 1950 the architect T. Shirley Worthington

First phase of the Library, 1974 (Photograph: University of Leicester)

David Wilson Library, 2008

of Thomas Worthington & Sons, Manchester was commissioned to design a new library.

The new brick two-storey building under a lightweight steel supported copper roof, bisected the original quadrangle of the Fielding Johnson Building, connecting the two main wings with the original chapel, thus creating the two smaller courtyards as seen today. When officially opened in 1954 the new library only occupied part of the new building. It served as the University Library when the charter was sealed on 1 May 1957 and by 1960 it had expanded to fill the whole Worthington extension.

A new purpose-built library was therefore commissioned by the University from Castle Park Dean & Hook architects. The brief was for an 8000m² air-conditioned building with a linear plan to permit further extensions as the University increased in size. It was completed by the contractors Marshall-Andrew & Co. Ltd. in 1974 as the first of three phases, and officially opened in September 1975 by the poet and former member of the library staff, Philip Larkin. The building, of reinforced concrete construction, was characterised by the reflective dark glass curtain wall which had become fashionable following the Foster Associates Willis Faber and Dumas building in Ipswich, which is characterised by a wavy

Interior details

glass façade creating interesting reflections across the street. The University library building was entered through well-designed projecting drum doors under a space-frame canopy. It was given a Royal Institute of British Architects East Midlands Regional Architectural Award.

The anticipated second and third phases of the library were delayed until in 2004, when Associated Architects, Birmingham were commissioned to prepare a planning design statement for the extension and refurbishment of the 1974 library to a state-of-the-art building fulfilling anticipated academic requirements of the new century. The design criteria included the requirement for a light and welcoming building with an appropriate sense of place and visual interest, linking seamlessly into the 1974 building. Additionally the building should be durable, economical to run and clear in its organisation.

The library is named after David Wilson, the house builder, who donated £2m towards the £25m construction costs. The building with an in-situ reinforced concrete frame and precast concrete flooring units is characterised by the sequence of atrium spaces down the central spine admitting light into the deep plan building. The entrance atrium is a sophisticated combination of glass and steel

giving a very modern access via a stainless steel doorway to a state-of-the-art library. The internal atria are softened with exposed timber to give a cool appropriately 'academic' feel to the core, which acts as the airy circulation space with the book stacks, computing facilities, quiet reading spaces and specialist accommodation being located around the perimeter.

'Flying Colours'
by Almuth Tebbenhoff, 2008

The library is enhanced by the incorporation of two sculptures by Helaine Blumenfeld entitled Shadow Figures – Dialogue. The first, in resin, (2003) is located in the rear atrium linking through to the original Fielding Johnson Building. The second, in bronze, (2008) is located in the main atrium as a central feature to give the library an appropriate air of gravitas. The entrance zone has the suspended work of art 'Flying Colours' by Almuth Tebbenhoff.

'Shadow Figures – Dialogue'
by Helaine Blumenfeld,
2003 (far left); 2008 (left)

Externally the building pays homage to its surroundings. The front glazed façade, as with the 1974 Castle Park Dean & Hook building, creates interesting reflections from the James Stirling Engineering Building.

The other elevations empathise with the Fielding Johnson Building. The original 1974 buff brickwork of the elevation near to the Fielding Johnson building is retained, whilst the extension and new work is finished in similarly coloured buff ceramic rain screen cladding and buff precast concrete panels.

In 1974 glazing technology had not achieved its current level of sophistication, therefore the first building phase suffered from overheating in the summer and heavy heat losses in the winter. The upgrading of the existing building has addressed these issues, to ensure that the whole library has appropriate energy consumption commensurate with current standards.

Natural daylight is admitted through extensive glazing which necessarily requires solar control to prevent overheating. The new south-east elevation has a ventilated triple glazing system, whilst solar shading devices are located on the south-west and north-west elevations.

The new extension, like the 1974 building, requires air handling units which are now visually screened on the roof. Energy management systems including heat recovery minimise energy use. In addition, in order to reduce the overall energy requirement for the building, an array of photovoltaic cells is located over the south-west atrium adjacent to the Fielding Johnson Building.

Main entrance

Photovoltaic panels

'Flight'
by Helaine Blumenfeld, 2014

In addition to providing accommodation for the university academic library functions, the building has a café. The quality of the building was acknowledged by winning the RIBA (Royal Institute of British Architects) East Midlands Awards for Architecture 2008 and also the ProCon (Property and Construction in Leicestershire) Building of the Year Award 2008.

In May 2012, a large underground cycle park, constructed by Danaher Walsh Civil Engineers under the podium to the front of the David Wilson Library, was officially opened. The park accommodates 300 bikes using a Josta two-tier racking system. The courtyard over the cycle park is enhanced by a seating area incorporating a sculpture entitled 'Flight' by Helaine Blumenfeld.

The University of Leicester was honoured by Her Majesty The Queen and HRH The Duke of Edinburgh who on an official visit to Leicester on 4 December 2008 formally opened the new library.

The Official Opening
(Photograph: The University of Leicester)

Sir Peter Williams introduces Her Majesty The Queen to Pro-Vice-Chancellor Christine Fyfe (centre) and Ms Louise Jones, Director of Library Services (left) (Photograph: The University of Leicester)

Her Majesty The Queen and HRH The Duke of Edinburgh with the Vice-Chancellor Professor Sir Robert Burgess and the Chancellor Sir Peter Williams CBE, FRS (Photograph: The University of Leicester)

Central Research Facility

The £16m Central Research Facility gives space for biomedical research including laboratories, and an MRI machine. The building houses vital research into the understanding, treatment and potential cure of a wide range of serious health problems including heart and kidney diseases, cancer, meningitis and diabetes. The building is used by researchers from different university departments.

The building, designed by Capita Symonds and constructed by Willmott Dixon was completed in August 2011 and officially opened on 28 September 2012 by Sir Peter Soulsby, Mayor of the City of Leicester.

Centre for Medicine

The £4.2m Centre for Medicine, located on the corner of Regent Road and University Road, was designed according to Passivhaus principles by Associated Architects and constructed by Willmott Dixon. It is the largest building in the UK built to Passivhaus standards ensuring that little additional energy is required for heating or cooling. The building with sections of 3, 4 and 5 floors incorporates high thermal mass, a green wall and roof, highly insulated and air-tight fabric, triple glazing and photo-voltaic panels.

Fresh air for the building is passed through a heat exchanger which is maintained at a constant 16 degrees centigrade by the 1.6 km array of pipework 2m below the building. Additional heating is drawn from the university's district heating system. Active and passive shading prevents summer overheating, whilst maximizing internal daylighting levels.

The Centre for Medicine completed in 2016 has accommodation for the Leicester Medical School and the Departments of Medical & Social Care Education, Health Sciences and Neuroscience, Psychology & Behaviour. It provides teaching rooms, academic offices and atrium spaces to encourage community engagement.

The landscaped forecourt of the building will incorporate a sculpture entitled 'Renewal' by Diane Maclean, which has a snake at its centre symbolising healing and medicine.

Green wall

Green wall detail

Atrium

South Campus

Freemen's Cottages

Roof detail

Freemen's Cottages, 161 Welford Road are Grade II listed Victorian properties which accommodate a range of student support services.

The first buildings were constructed in 1856. Subsequently in 1883 the architects, Redfern and Sawday drew up plans for a large rear extension, but these plans were then modified by Stockdale Harrison in 1885. The modified proposal included recessed bays for beds in each room, taking a foot off the width of the spine corridor. The front porch to the centre of the street façade was retained in the Redfern and Sawday drawings, but converted to store cupboards in the Stockdale Harrison proposals. Clearly it was then totally removed. The 1885 additions were constructed by the builder H. Bland, who also built the Clephan Building for De Montfort University at much

the same time. The contiguous building to the left was designed by Stockdale Harrison and constructed in 1893 by J. Hutchinson & Son, with Thomas Parsons as the overseer. Originally the two houses were separated by a pathway.

It is believed that grazing rights on Freemen's Common dated back to Simon de Montfort. A large area of Freemen's Common was sold to the University for student accommodation in 1967.

South Campus Halls

The Freemen's Common Houses were built in 1975.

Freemen's Common Houses

The original Nixon Court was designed in two phases by the Douglas Smith Stimson Partnership and completed in 1993 and 1994 respectively as 'Design and Build' contracts in collaboration with J.H. Hallam (Contracts) Ltd. The Hall is named after Sir Edwin Nixon CBE, who was Chairman of Council (1992-1998) and Pro-Chancellor of the University (1995-1998).

Nixon Court - Putney Road

Nixon Court

Additions to Nixon Court designed by Architects Design Partnership and built by Willmott Dixon Housing Ltd were completed in September 2011.The additions give significant increases to the university student accommodation on the South Campus with close access to the Central Campus.

Nixon Court

North Campus

School of Education

The centre of the School of Education is accommodated on University Road in three large converted houses linked together by the former education library and assembly hall designed by Douglas Smith, and built in 1966 by Johnson & Bailey Ltd. The 1960s building is a concrete frame with a white tile façade similar to the Adrian Building of the same era. Concrete columns are partially exposed. The three Victorian houses were stripped of their outbuildings to provide the space for the 1966 linking building.

On completion of the David Wilson Library, education material was centralised and the former education library space is now re-configured for Museum Studies.

Museum Studies Building, 1966

School of Education –
21 University Road

School of Education – 21 University Road
(Princess Road East elevation)

Number 21 University Road is a significant example of English Vernacular style architecture, designed in 1872 by Jackson and Heazell of Bromley House, Market Place, Nottingham and developed in 1873, for Henry Smith. The pair of semi-detached villas is notable for its circular tower and conical slate roof. The larger house had an entrance on to Princess Road, and the smaller property used the current building entrance, sideways on to Victoria Road, now University Road. The larger property has an unspoilt c.1910 Art Nouveau fireplace that was uncovered from inside a walled storeroom.

Number 15 University Road on the corner of New Walk and Victoria Road, as it was named at that time, was designed by W. Jackson, and built by 1872 for Mr George Lucas. The property was initially named

Rutland House and George Lucas is described in the local directories as a 'fancy draper'. The house was subsequently extended and the roofline modified.

School of Education –
15 University Road

Additional facilities for the School of Education are located in 2 University Road and the adjacent Fraser Noble Building. Number 2 University Road was designed for Joseph Harvey, solicitor of Joseph and Robert Harvey by Stockdale Harrison in 1878. It was completed in 1879. The newel post carries the initials J.H. and date 1879. Benjamin Burrows, the musician had a studio in this building as recorded by the blue plaque.

School of Education –
2 University Road

Fraser Noble Building –
London Road

The Fraser Noble Building comprises the Edward Wood Hall, initially known as the Victoria Road Institute. It was designed by G. Lawton Brown, founded in c.1909 and opened by the Mayor of London, Dr John Clifford in 1910. Earlier work is to the rear. The building was purchased by the University in 1985 to provide computing facilities, science laboratories and seminar rooms. Sir Edward Wood was four times Mayor of Leicester, given the Freedom of the Borough in 1896, and was knighted in 1906. Sir T.A. Fraser Noble MBE was Vice-Chancellor of the University from 1962 to 1976 and was knighted in 1971.

North Campus Houses

The North Campus consists of a range of elegant Victorian houses that have been converted to university use. The buildings are located on Regent Road, University Road, Upper New Walk, Princess Road and Salisbury Road; a selection is illustrated.

Salisbury Road Houses

1 Salisbury Road, dated 1878, was designed for Squire of the Morgan Squire (now Fenwick) Department Store, Leicester by R.J. and J. Goodacre. Goodacre also designed the adjacent pair of semi-detached houses, numbered 3 and 5 in 1877. Number 5 was initially occupied by George Padmore of the hosiery manufacturers G. & J.W. Padmore, and it was subsequently extended to the rear in 1893 by Sharp, the builder. Finally the north side of the road was completed with a further pair of Goodacre villas, Numbers 7 and 9, in 1884, probably as speculative development by the architect.

Marc Fitch Historical Institute,
1 Salisbury Road

The Marc Fitch Historical Institute occupies 1, 3 and 5 Salisbury Road. Marcus Fitch CBE established in 1956 an educational charity to support historical research focussed on regional and local history. He later endowed the Salisbury Road building with funds to convert it to its current use incorporating his personal library. Marc Fitch died in 1994.

Marc Fitch Historical Institute,
3 - 5 Salisbury Road

'Diversity in Harmony'
by Naomi Blake c.1990
9 Salisbury Road

Centre for Medical Humanities,
7 Salisbury Road

Centre for Systems Neuroscience,
9 Salisbury Road

On the south side of the road, in 1879 Goddard and Paget developed a pair of semi-detached villas, now numbered 12 and 14, for John Hodges of T.W. Hodges, elastic web manufacturer. The following year the architect James Tait built the terrace of five houses, with the even numbers from 2 to 10, for William Stanyon, a boot and shoe manufacturer. These properties, including Number 6, now owned by the University, were let to tenants. Finally in 1881, John Hodges, with another Goddard and Paget design, developed the property on the corner of Regent Road adjacent to his Number 14. In some early documentation this part of Salisbury Road is referred to as Salisbury Street, which now is the name only for the section of the road to the east of New Walk.

6 Salisbury Road

14 Salisbury Road

Regent Road

Regent Road has a selection of elegant 19th century properties. Numbers 114-116 (not part of the University) and 118-120 Regent Road are two very similar semi-detached villas. The adjacent Number 112 Regent Road is clearly dated 1871. For a period towards the end if the nineteenth century, 120 Regent Road was occupied by William Gimson of Gimson & Sons, the Leicester timber merchants.

118 - 120 Regent Road, c.1870

Number 128 Regent Road, a substantial residence on the corner of Regent Road and University Road was designed by Joseph Goddard in 1873 for F. Hodges, although at that time University Road was still known as Victoria Road. It is now occupied by the Vaughan Centre for Lifelong Learning.

128 Regent Road

Vaughan Centre for Lifelong Learning,
128 Regent Road

The Vaughan Centre for Lifelong Learning evolved from Vaughan College which originated as a 'Working Men's College' with reading room facilities in Union Street, Leicester in 1862. The college moved to purpose built premises in 1908, when it was officially named as 'The Vaughan Working Men's College and Institute', after Canon David James Vaughan, Vicar of St Martin's Parish Church (now Leicester Cathedral). In 1962, Vaughan College for Lifelong Learning moved to new premises designed by Trevor Dannatt at the Jewry Wall Museum, but this accommodation was sold to the Leicester Museum Service in 2015 and the Vaughan Centre moved to Regent Road.

The Second Vaughan College Building (1908)
(Photograph: University of Leicester Archive)

University Road

Number 6 University Road named 'Carisbrooke' was designed in 1896 for George Owston Marshall by T.W. Pettifor of Leicester. Marshall was a house agent and auctioneer, but also a churchwarden and treasurer to St Martin's Cathedral in Leicester. Unusually for that period, the house had a photographic dark room in the top storey. It is now occupied by the School of Achaeology and Ancient History, the School of Education and the Society for Libyan Studies Archive.

6 University Road

Princess Road East

The local architect Joseph Goddard designed many of the houses on the south side of Princess Road East between University Road and West Walk. The street was built from c.1880. The ornate wooden porch on the 105 Princess Road East, is one of a few of very similar design within the area.

University Squash Courts,
111A Princess Road East

School of Education,
School of Social Work,
107 Princess Road East

Leicester Learning Institute,
105 Princess Road East

105 Princess Road East

Upper New Walk

Numbers 152 and 154 Upper New Walk were designed by Stockdale Harrison for clients Davis and Witham, and are characterised by the brick, stone and timber detailing associated with elegant turrets, gables and bay windows. 154 Upper New Walk is named 'The Friars' and was built in 1888, whilst 152 Upper New Walk was constructed in 1889. The Friars was occupied by Samuel Davis, manager of the Permanent Building Society and the Freehold Land Society, whilst number 152 was occupied by Aldersleigh Edward Witham, a pawnbroker. These buildings are now occupied by the Department of Criminology.

Department of Criminology, 152-154 Upper New Walk

152 Upper New Walk

154 Upper New Walk

154 Upper New Walk, Wyvern Finial

Stoneygate

Brookfield

Brookfield is situated approximately two miles east of the city centre, just off the London Road leading from Victoria Park. The centre-piece of the campus, within mature gardens, is Brookfield House which was rebuilt in 1877, when it was sold by the Burgess family to Mr Johnson T. Fielding JP. He employed the architects Joseph Goddard and Alfred H. Paget to design the present building. Its half-timbered construction with stone-mullioned and transomed windows and grey brickwork was the earliest example of timber-framed revival within nineteenth century Leicester. The rainwater downpipe heads bear the initials J.T.F. and date 1877. Stone medallions also bear the initials J.T.F. Johnson Thomas Fielding, whose name is strongly linked with the University of Leicester, remained resident at Brookfield House until his death in 1922. The elegant central stair hall is lit by a lantern, and all original fixtures and fittings, including decorative glass, are of a very high quality.

For a brief period from 1922 to 1926, the house was occupied by the Archdeacon of Loughborough, William Phillip, who temporarily renamed the property Merrivale.

Some alterations were made to the kitchen in 1926, by the following resident, Rev C. Bardsley, Bishop of Leicester. Subsequently, the stable block was converted to workshops, and when the bishop died in 1946 the buildings were passed to the Royal Infirmary as a training school. The transfer was not entirely smooth, as Fielding Johnson had set up a trust in his will, donating the house to the Leicester Diocese as the Bishop's residence if required,

Brookfield House

Rear porch

Central stair

Front door glazing

or if this was not accepted, it should be gifted to the Infirmary. When the building was no longer required by the diocese, they argued that it should then be sold not donated to the Infirmary, as according to the terms of the will they had accepted

the original gift. Eventually the Infirmary governors paid £10,000 for the house as a training school for nurses.

The original outbuildings, including the caretaker's cottage and the stable block are all contemporary

with the 1877 refurbished Brookfield House, and illustrate the attention to detail characteristic of the Goddard and Paget architectural practice.

Further alterations were made in 1955 and the additional accommodation including Heron

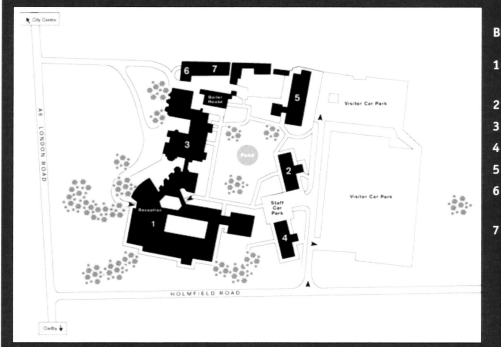

Brookfield

1 Postgraduate Training Centre
2 Mallard House
3 Brookfield House
4 Heron House
5 Kingfisher House
6 Mary Seacole House
7 Stable Block

Mary Seacole House

House, Mallard House, Kingfisher House and the Postgraduate Training Centre, designed by Leslie Conway of the Trent Regional Health Authority's Architects' Department were completed by 1975. The adjacent additions nearest to Brookfield House were designed as a small-scale series of linked one-storey pavilions in grey-brown brick and white weatherboarding, thus leaving the dominance of the original house.

Other red and brown brick buildings are placed within the context of the seven-acre mature gardens of Brookfield House.

Stable Block

Brookfield was formerly the Charles Frears Campus of De Montfort University and was named after Charles Russell Frears, who was a leading campaigner for appropriate maternity facilities in Leicester, which led to the development of a new maternity unit at the Leicester Royal Infirmary. Charles Frears was managing director of Frears Biscuits Limited, which was taken over by the

American National Biscuit Company in 1963. He was Chairman of Leicester No.1 Hospital Management Committee from 1963 to 1972, and in this capacity supported the development of the Medical School at the University of Leicester and the redevelopment of Brookfield House as a School of Nursing, which was duly named after him in 1975. The Charles Frears College of Nursing merged with De Montfort University in 1995 and now this discipline has been relocated to Edith Murphy House on De Montfort University's city campus. Brookfield was sold to the University of Leicester in 2013.

Charles Frears was one of the longest serving members of the University of Leicester Council and its preceding University College Council. He was particularly interested in the Botanic Garden, giving a collection of rare botanical books to the College and supporting the move of the University Botanic Garden from Leicester to Oadby.

Mary Seacole House is named after Mary Seacole, a Jamaican-born nurse of Scottish and Jamaican parentage who, with considerable knowledge of tropical medicines from her mother, travelled at her own expense to the Crimean War to assist the injured from both sides of the conflict.

It is appropriate that Brookfield House, once owned by Johnson T. Fielding, who gave the university its first building is now back in the ownership of the University of Leicester. The buildings house the Postgraduate Training Centre and sections of the university administration.

Heron House

Kingfisher House

Knighton

Knighton Hall

Knighton Hall Stables

Knighton Hall, the President and Vice-Chancellor's official residence is detailed in Pevsner. The two-storey building constructed over several centuries is coordinated by the mellow brickwork and rusticated stone quoins. The early part, built in the early eighteenth century, consists of small four bays. The windows are featured with moulded stone surrounds and emphasised keystones, and the roof obscured by a tall parapet. However, this façade conceals late sixteenth century work visible in the interior, and the rear of the house has a different character being gabled and roughcast, with wooden mullioned windows.

The centre of the façade, incorporating the semi-circular porch, was built in the late eighteenth or early nineteenth century, and according to Pevsner, probably by John Johnson. A further single-storey extension was added in the twentieth century, stylistically to mirror the original façade.

The house, and the separate stables dated 1837, are set in well-maintained mature gardens, part of which were used for the construction by Trevor Dannatt of College Hall in 1960.

The Knighton Hall estate was acquired by Edmund Cradock in 1719, and it remained in the name of Cradock through direct and indirect descent to Edward Cradock, who was principal of Brasenose College, Oxford in 1880. The Cradock family rarely used Knighton Hall as a residence. It was leased to John Shipley Ellis in the 1850s, rented out to William Wilkins Vincent, a hat manufacturer between 1880 and 1920 and to the Oram family until 1946 when it was purchased by Councillor Charles Keene. In 1947 it was sold to the University College for a women's hall of residence, but it became the official residence of the President and Vice-Chancellor.

Nearby, the two hectare Attenborough Arboretum and Education Centre was opened by Sir David Attenborough CH, CVO, CBE, FRS in 1997. The arboretum illustrates a portion of medieval ridge-and-furrow field, ponds and a planting scheme of native trees in

'Spring and Autumn' by Anthony Ankers, 1997

the sequence in which they arrived into this country following the last ice age approximately 10,000 years ago. The arboretum also features a sculpture 'Spring and Autumn' by Anthony Ankers.

College Court

College Court in Knighton was designed by Trevor Dannatt and Sir Leslie Martin in 1957 as one of the main halls of residence for the university. It was completed in 1960 as College Hall. The building consisted of five Grade II-listed two and three storey buildings which offered 180-bed student accommodation and garaging. The building complex, constructed in pale buff brickwork around courtyard spaces, has a collegiate style described by Trevor Dannatt himself as 'unemotional'. The hall has a strong empathy with the low-rise main university campus buildings of the same period. The building was reopened after a major refurbishment in 2013 as a residential conference centre and events venue.

The modernised College Court, designed by Associated Architects and constructed by Wilmott Dixon, has 123 bedrooms, public and private dining facilities, bar and a range of conference rooms. The buildings are located within three acres of mature landscaped gardens adjacent to the Attenborough Arboretum.

College Court – Front Entrance

Dining Room

Conference Facilities

Mary Gee Houses

The Mary Gee houses are located on Ratcliffe Road in the Knighton district of Leicester, about 2km from the central campus. They consist of 36 three-storey houses each with ten study bedrooms.

The complex, completed in two phases in 1971 and 1972, was constructed by William Davis (Leicester) Ltd. as Design and Build packages, to a performance specification by the University.

Mary Gee was the second wife of Percy Gee, whom he married when his first wife died. Mary and Percy had been prevented from marrying earlier as she was from a clerical professional family, whereas he was from a trade background, albeit the very successful shoe company Stead and Simpson, of which he was chairman. Percy Gee died a month after Mary Elinor Gee in 1962. In his will he donated their residence (Birnam House on the corner of Elms Road and Ratcliffe Road) and the land for the current student accommodation to the University on the condition that it was named after his late wife, Mary.

Oadby Student Village
Halls of Residence

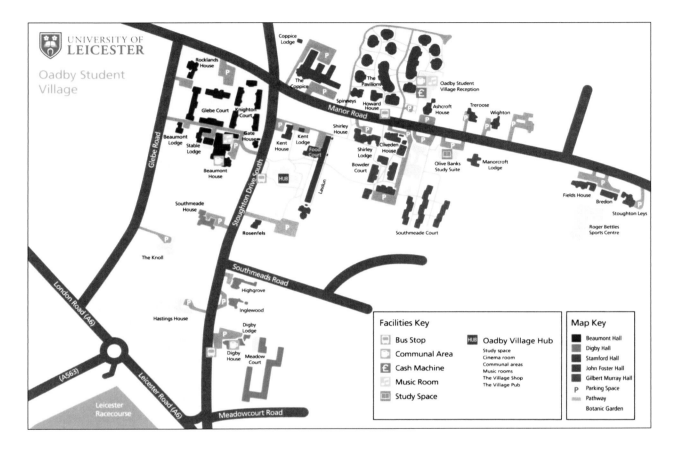

(Plan: University of Leicester)

The University possesses a significant number of elegant Edwardian and inter-war houses in Oadby which together form a large community of student housing. Some of the properties have been extended, whilst others have had new buildings constructed within former gardens. The properties are predominantly located on Manor Road, Glebe Road and Stoughton Drive South and many were designed by the major architectural practices of the period, particularly Stockdale Harrison & Sons, but also Ralph Bedingfield and Lawton Brown. The houses were commissioned largely by industrialists, particularly owners of hosiery and footwear companies, for which Leicester was famous. The houses and newer developments are grouped into five main clusters, namely, Beaumont Hall, Digby Hall, Stamford Hall, John Foster Hall and Gilbert Murray Hall, but not all buildings are illustrated.

Beaumont Hall

Originally named Middlemeade, the 'Arts and Crafts' Beaumont House with paired gables and sweeping tiled roofs was designed by Stockdale Harrison in 1904 for Frank S. Brice, a hosiery manufacturer, who sold it on to S.H. Driver, who was also a hosiery manufacturer in Leicester. Middlemeade was sold to the University and renamed Beaumont Hall in 1947, when Shirley Worthington, the University architect at the time, was commissioned to make significant additions to the property.

The first phase of University development was the restrained Neo-Georgian housing and dining hall designed by T. Shirley Worthington and built by William Morris & Sons in 1950.

The second phase of development designed by Shirley Worthington and built by Chitham & Co. Ltd. reflects its 1962 vintage.

On the corner of Glebe Road and Manor Road is Rocklands, which was built in 1902 for William Barrow, a brick manufacturer.

Beaumont House
Panelled Entrance Hall

Beaumont House

Knighton Court

Glebe Court

Rocklands

Digby Hall

Digby House

Digby House was originally named Meadowcourt and built in 1908 for Thomas J. Thorneloe in 'Jacobethan' style by Stockdale Harrison & Sons. It was bought by the University in 1949 and extended to the east by Richard Sheppard, Robson & Partners in 1962 to provide communal facilities and student accommodation blocks.

Meadow Court

Hastings House was built in 1902 for W.H. Stevens JP as Nether Close by Stockdale and Shirley Harrison. The house was renamed Hastings House when purchased by the University in 1947. Hastings House is constructed of Leicestershire keuper marl clay bricks, with their orange-red colour contrasting to the timberwork and stone detailing in a composition recalling the 17th century. The featured gables and dormer windows to the clay tiled roof render a vernacular character to the house. The mature conifers, now part of the Botanic Garden, were planted by the original owner.

Hastings House

Hastings House

The Knoll

The Knoll was built in 1907 for William H. Winterton, the owner of the Gipsy Lane Leicester brickworks, whose interest is reflected in the Elizabethan styling incorporating diaper patterns in the hand-made brickwork. It was designed for him by his architect nephew William Henry Bidlake of Birmingham. William Bidlake had connections with the Leicester architects Tait and Goddard who nominated him for a Fellowship of the RIBA (Royal Institute of British Architects) in 1922. The roof is of local Swithland slate. The entrance hall is panelled with a low-relief white frieze depicting the Seven Graces. The second owner was E.S. Fox of Fox's Glacier Mints, and ultimately The Knoll was purchased from Mrs Fox by the University in 1964.

The Knoll: Rainwater Head (above right), Entrance Hall (below) & The Seven Graces Decorative Frieze (left)

Inglewood

Inglewood of brick and render construction was built in 1904 for John Alfred Sabin a local footwear manufacturer. In 1915 a 'motor house' designed by Seale and Riley of Leicester was added and in 1936 the house was extended for J.A. Sabin by the builder H.M. Dudgeon. It was purchased by the University in 1960.

Southmeade

Southmeade was built in 1927 for Francis Strange Brice, the hosiery manufacturer, by Stockdale Harrison & Sons, although to a more restrained Neo-Georgian style than their earlier works. It was built in the original grounds of Beaumont House formerly Middlemeade when F.S. Brice sold Middlemeade to S.H. Driver.

Highgrove

Highgrove built to 'Jacobethan' style with red brick and tile, articulated by stone transom and mullioned windows and entrance, was constructed in 1905 for T.S. Grieve who was a manufacturer of machinery components. A 'motor house' designed by Seale and Riley of Leicester was added in 1914.

Stamford Hall

Stamford House

Stamford House – lead detail

Stamford House was originally named Cartmel Close and was built in 1907 by Stockdale Harrison & Sons. The clients initials J.B. and P.L.B., together with the date, are embossed on leadwork, although subsequent additions to the original house almost obscure them. P.L.Baker was a tobacco dealer. A garage by H.L. Goddard and W.A. Catlow of Leicester was added in 1916, when the house was listed under the name Highbury. It was purchased by the University in 1964 and is now the Oadby Village Hub, with shop, pub, cinema and communal areas.

Lasdun was designed by Sir Denys Lasdun and built in 1964 by Johnson & Bailey Ltd. The building is characterised by the tiled mono-pitched roofs incorporating terraces and the randomly located vertical slit windows. The building has much of the characteristics of Denys Lasdun's three-storey student accommodation at Fitzwilliam College, Cambridge.

Kent House

Kent House with rendered walls and a tiled roof was originally named One Oak. It was designed in 1902 by Stockdale and Shirley Harrison and built for Arthur Whitmore, a wholesale grocer. The house is characterised by its extensive loggia running into the two-storey facetted bay. The property was subsequently occupied by Mrs C.A. Broadbent who in 1925 planned additional upper storey bays to a design by Baines and Provins of Leicester. One Oak and Nether Close (now Hastings House) were the first houses to be developed in this area of Oadby. It was purchased by the University in 1956.

Rosenfels, in white render under a tiled roof, was built in 1907 for T.D. Meakin of the hosiery trade. It was sold to the University in 1968 by F.N. Parker, who had previously in 1933 added a garage designed by Brand and Edwards of Leicester.

Rosenfels

John Foster Hall

John Foster Pavilions

John Foster Hall, designed by Goddard Manton and built by J.H. Hallam, was completed in 2006 on the site formerly occupied by the Villiers Hall accommodation which had been built by Castle and Park in 1967. The Hall was named and officially opened by John C. Foster OBE, former Chairman of Council and Pro-Chancellor of the University in 2007. Adjacent to John Foster Hall is Ashcroft House, originally the residence of J. Leeson, which was altered slightly in 1916 by W.L. Keites, T.H. Fosbrooke and W.K. Bedingfield. To the left of the John Foster Pavilions is Howard House which was originally named The Homestead and occupied by Sydney Tyler a shoe manufacturer.

Ashcroft House

Howard House

Treroose

Treroose, characterised by its three-storey gables and white rendered walls expressed at the corners as quoins, was built in 1922 for W. Bertie Jarvis who was in the hosiery business. The additional garage was designed in 1922 by Clement C. Ogden. The adjacent house, Wighton, was built in 1908 for Francis Graham Langmore of Castle's Brewery. In 1929, a ground floor bay and verandah were added to the design by Cowdell and Bryan of Leicester.

Wighton

The Spinneys

The Spinneys in red brick and slate Tudor Gothic style was designed by Lawton Brown and built in 1905 for F.M. Waite, the manager of Barclays Bank in Gallowtree Gate, Leicester.

The Beeches was designed in 1920 by James Stockdale Harrison and built by William Moss of Loughborough for Colonel Herbert Johnson Burnham who was a hosiery manufacturer in Oadby. The L-shaped Neo-Georgian property under a hipped tiled roof is enlivened by the two varieties of coloured brick which were brought from Tring in Hertfordshire. The house was eventually bought by the University in 1957.

The Beeches

The Coppice

The Coppice, on the corner of Stoughton Drive South and Manor Road, was built for W.H. Tomlinson, a shoe manufacturer. The associated lodge on Stoughton Drive South designed by Clement C. Ogden was built in 1923. The property was purchased by Leicester Education Authority in 1949 and converted into student accommodation for the Leicester Colleges of Art and Technology. The house was extended with a north wing designed by J.H. Lloyd Owen, the City Architect in 1951 and further extended to the east by the city architects in 1953. The building was eventually transferred from De Montfort University to the University of Leicester as part of the Oadby Student Village.

Gilbert Murray Hall

Gilbert Murray House was originally named Villiers House. It was designed by T. Henry Bowell of Leicester for C.H. Roberts in 1921. Roberts was the owner of Portland Shoes and his factory building on De Montfort University's campus retains the Portland name. The House was renamed in 1957 after Professor Gilbert Murray of Oxford University, who had been the University 'Visitor' since 1929.

Gilbert Murray House

Stamford Court

Stamford Court was designed by Leonard Manasseh & Partners and built in 1966 by Johnson & Bailey Ltd. It was refurbished and officially reopened as a conference centre in September 2012.

Stamford Court

Clivedon

Clivedon, built in 1907, was occupied by J.R. Fitzmaurice in 1916, when Roberts had a summer house designed by Clement Stretton built in the Villiers House (Gilbert Murray House) garden. A garage designed by Baines and Provins was added to Clivedon in 1919.

Clivedon

Southmeade Court – Wistow Block

Southmeade Court was designed by Leonard Manasseh & Partners and built in 1966 by Johnson & Bailey Ltd.

Southmeade Court

Olive Banks

The Olive Banks Study Suite, formerly
Manorcroft was built in 1928 for
Ernest Lillie, a company director,
by Ralph W. Bedingfield. The house
is characterised by the alternating
white render and herringbone
brickwork to the bays. Bedingfield
taught for several years at the
Leicester School of Architecture,
now De Montfort University. He
was influenced by the architecture
of Voysey and this is visible in the
distinctive white rendered walls,
roof styling and fenestration. Olive
Banks was Professor of Sociology in
the University from 1973-82. She is
noted for her work on the sociology of
education and the history of feminism.

Bredon

Bredon, with its prominent almost
Flemish gable, was designed in 1924
by George Nott and G.A. Cope. George
Nott was the Head of the School of
Architecture at the Art School, now
De Montfort University. He taught
part-time and ran a practice on
New Walk. The first owner of this
unusual design was J.R. Potts who
was managing director of Downing
& Sons hosiery manufacturer.
The house was purchased by the
University in 1950. To the right, the
adjacent property, Fields House, was
designed in 1922 by H.H. Thomson
& Co. of Leicester for H.D. Greenlees
the shoe manufacturer, who named
the property Saigon. The property
was subsequently named Tetuan by
the next owner, John Adams Bolton
and eventually sold to the University
in 1962.

Olive Banks

Bredon

Fields House

Stoughton Leys

Stoughton Leys, adjacent to Bredon, was designed in 1923 by G. Lawton Brown and Percy C. Jones for Mrs Clara Pochin. It was purchased by the University in 1953.

Shirley House was originally named Sorrrento and was built in 1906 for Robert Hyslop a footwear manufacturer. The building with a hint of 'Art & Crafts' style is characterised by the deep gables, and to the first floor; tile hanging and decorative wood carving to the window heads.

Shirley House

Shirley House – decoration

Shirley Lodge, delicate in scale, was built in 1906 at the same time as Sorrento.

Shirley Lodge

Bowder Court was completed in 1992 by Jonathan Smith & Partners as a Design and Build contract in collaboration with Monk Construction (later Trafalgar House).

The Court is named after Dr Kenneth W. Bowder OBE, Pro-Chancellor 1978 – 1991 and Chairman of Council 1981-1991.

Bowder Court

University Botanic Garden, Oadby

The University Botanic Garden originated on the Main Campus to the south-west side of the Fielding Johnson Building. The idea of a Botanic Garden was first mooted in 1920, and by 1925 it comprised a herb garden, medicinal plants, a rock and water garden, together with a woodland garden of the local Charnwood flora. Maintenance was variable and in 1935 it was described in committee as 'a weedy rock garden', but in 1937 a new initiative arose from the Botany Department to develop further the Botanic Garden.

Pre-war Botanic Garden
(Photograph: The University of
Leicester, Brian Burch)

In 1947 the Botanic Garden was moved to its current 6.5 hectare site in the combined gardens of Beaumont House, Southmeade, The Knoll and Hastings House. Many mature trees date back to the early twentieth century when the gardens for these elegant Edwardian houses were laid out and maintained by teams of gardeners. Beaumont House had a sandstone garden developed by the original owner, and a limestone garden was added in c.1930. By 1968, the boundaries between the four separate gardens had been removed.

The Harold Martin Botanic Garden now incorporates herbaceous borders, rock gardens, a herb garden, an arboretum and various formal gardens with a pool and pergolas. Glasshouses display cacti, succulents, tropical and alpine plants. In particular, the gardens are home to part of the National Council for the Conservation of Plants and Gardens (NCCPG) Hardy Fuchsia Collection.

A range of sculptures are on permanent display within the gardens. The botanic garden is named after H.B. Martin who was Secretary and Registrar to the University College from 1947 to 1957.

Permanent Display - 'Hybrid' by Deirdre Hubbard FRBS, Hon D.Litt University of Leicester, 2001

'Epistrophe', Tony Long, late 1960s

Roger Bettles Sports Centre, Oadby

The University's Roger Bettles Sports Centre is located on the Manor Road, Oadby sports ground. The building designed by Brimelow McSweeney Architects and constructed by Bowmer & Kirkland opened in the autumn of 2012. The building has a 25m swimming pool, sauna and steam rooms, a spa pool, a large gym and aerobics studio together with changing facilities. The new building is linked through a glass passage to the earlier sports hall which was opened by David Gower in October 1987.

Roger Bettles Sports Centre

Entrance Foyer

25m Swimming Pool

The fitness centre complements the external sporting facilities which include all-weather and floodlit soccer and rugby pitches, a running track and tennis courts. The centre is named after Roger Bettles who until recently was Chair of the University Council and Pro-Chancellor. The building was formally opened and named by Lord Grocott, Chancellor of the University of Leicester in September 2013. The University astronomical observatories are also on the sports field site.

Sports Hall

Astronomical Observatories
(1965 and 1980 [right])

Commercial Hall

Opal Court

Opal Court, 2007
(Opal Property Group)

Opal Court, designed by Stephen George and Partners is situated on Lancaster Road near to the University Central Campus.

De Montfort University
Buildings on the Campus

1. Art Factory
2. Bede Hall
3. Bede Island
4. Campus Centre
5. Chantry Building
6. Clephan Building
7. Edith Murphy House
8. Eric Wood Building
9. Estate Development Building
10. Estates Services Building
11. Filbert Village
    (private hall of residence)
12. Forensic Science Facility
13. Gateway House
14. Hawthorn Building
15. Heritage Centre
16. Heritage House
17. Hugh Aston Building
18. Innovation Centre
19. John Whitehead Building
20. Kimberlin Library
21. Leicester Castle Business School
22. Liberty Park
    (private hall of residence)
23. Mill Studios
24. Newarke Point
    (private hall of residence)
25. New Wharf Hall
26. PACE Building
27. Portland Building
28. Queen's Building
29. The Grange
    (private hall of residence)
30. The Greenhouse
31. Philip Tasker Building
32. Queen Elizabeth II Diamond Jubilee
    Leisure Centre
33. The Venue@DMU
34. Vijay Patel Building
35. Trinity House
36. Victoria Hall
    (private hall of residence)
37. Waterway Gardens
38. Watershed Centre
39. White Rose Cottage
40. 19 The Newarke
M   The Magazine Gateway

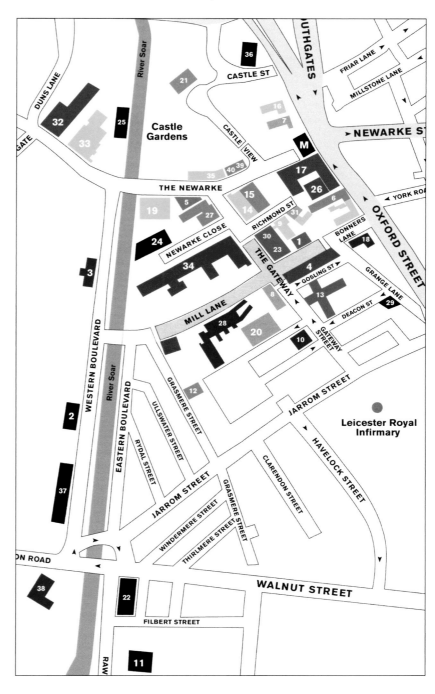

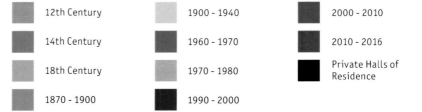

12th Century	1900 - 1940	2000 - 2010
14th Century	1960 - 1970	2010 - 2016
18th Century	1970 - 1980	Private Halls of Residence
1870 - 1900	1990 - 2000	

Leicester Castle

Leicester Castle, home of the Leicester Castle Business School, is a Listed Building, which has been leased by De Montfort University for 125 years from the Leicester City Council. It has recently undergone a major refurbishment with Maber Architects and Woodhead Construction to restore the building to its former glory within the historic Conservation Area.

Leicester Castle has a long and interesting history. The front façade, dated 1695, obscures a medieval hall built in the 12th century. Robert de Beaumont who became the 1st Earl of Leicester in 1107 started the replacement of the Norman wooden motte and bailey castle of 1068, and it is likely that his son, who became the 2nd Earl of Leicester in 1118, began the construction of the Great Hall in local sandstone. The interior was divided into a central nave with bay-divided side aisles all supported by an arcade of robust oak columns. One Norman scalloped timber capital from the original roof, which was covered with oak shingles, is preserved. Dendrochronology confirms that apart from the aisle posts, the building was reroofed following a survey in 1523. Some traces of original window positions can be seen. The large north window was replaced in 1821, but the original, in a similar position, would have been over the dais or high table. Stairs led up to the earl's private accommodation.

Castle – West facade overlooking Castle Park

Interior of the castle hall before 1821

(Photograph: Reproduced by permission of the Record Office for Leicestershire, Leicester and Rutland)

Norman column capital

The 16th century roof structure

Norman window (above)
Medieval doorway (below)

Criminal Court

Original Civil Court

In 1821 the Great Hall was divided into two separate court rooms with a cell block added in 1858. Additional facilities including private viewing galleries, barristers' and judges' rooms were created for each court. Court furniture incorporated included an emblazoned canopy over the judge's seat, a jury box, the dock and seating allocated to lawyers and witnesses.

Adjacent to the Great Hall is the vaulted John of Gaunt's cellar. It was reconstructed in c.1400 with an extension at the north end and the building of the present vaulted roof. Graffiti carved in 1798 show that it was used as a prison during the Napoleonic wars. It was probably originally built as storage for the castle kitchens.

Crown Court trials were held in the castle until 1992. The building, which is Listed Grade I for its interior and Grade II for its exterior, then remained unused until the heritage groups agreed with the major refurbishment now completed by the university.

John of Gaunt's cellar

Trinity House

The Trinity Hospital was founded by Henry Plantagenet, 3rd Earl of Lancaster and Leicester, in 1331 and dedicated in 'Honour of God and the Virgin Mary'. The original building consisted of a church to the east end, and accommodation to the west. It was well endowed by Earl Henry for fifty poor and infirm men to be cared for by five nurses under the management of a warden, four chaplains and two clerks. Twenty of the inmates were permanent residents, whilst the remaining thirty would leave after they had recovered their health. Earl Henry died in 1345 and he was buried in the hospital chapel in a service attended by Edward III and his Queen, Philippa of Hainault, Belgium.

In 1353, Earl Henry's son, Henry, the first Duke of Lancaster, raised the status of the Hospital to a College (St Mary the Great) and further endowed the establishment to a hundred poor and infirm men of whom forty would be permanent residents, under a dean, twelve canons, thirteen vicars, six choristers, three clerks and ten female nurses. The plan was also to build a collegiate church dedicated to 'The Annunciation of Our Lady', and when Henry, Duke of Lancaster died of the plague in 1361, the task was completed by his son-in-law John of Gaunt (Ghent). During his travels in Europe, the Duke of Lancaster was given a single thorn from the Christ's Crown of Thorns, a relic of great importance which had previously been enshrined by St Louis (Louis IX) at Sainte Chapelle,

Trinity Hospital, 1776
(Print: History and Antiquities of the County of Leicester, John Nichols)

Paris. This was given to the Collegiate Church and placed on the high alter as a focus of pilgrimage, but it was subsequently lost, possibly after the dissolution of the monasteries, when the Collegiate Church was surrendered to the Crown, dissolved in 1547 by Edward VI and subsequently demolished. The only remains of the Collegiate Church from 1590 are under the Hawthorn Building.

Fortunately, the hospital building survived and was given a new charter by James I in 1614/15 as 'The Hospital of the Holy Trinity in the Newarke'. It remained unchanged, although the fabric significantly deteriorated, until in 1776, during the reign of George III, the Derby architect, Joseph Pickford was commissioned to oversee the restoration. The south aisle was removed and the south arcade closed off as an external wall with windows. The main medieval infirmary hall was subdivided. One and a half of the original arches of the north arcade remain free-standing in the present entrance hall, whilst others are embedded in the subdivided hall. A second floor was added at this time to become

Trinity Hospital, 1796
(Print: History and Antiquities of the
County of Leicester, John Nichols)

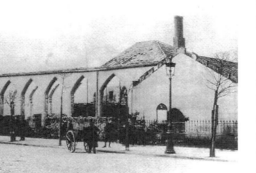

Trinity Hospital, 1901
(Photograph: Castle Park –
A Souvenir Guide, Leicester
County Council. Reproduced
by permission of the Record
Office for Leicestershire,
Leicester and Rutland)

the women's quarters and the lead roof covering was replaced with slates. The infilled Gothic arches to the chapel end are visible on both the Castle Mound and The Newarke façades.

In 1901, 100 feet of the residential part of the building was rebuilt to align to the new Newarke Bridge; the road having previously been a cul-de-sac. The replacement wing of the almshouse was designed in a style described by Pevsner as 'Jacobethan', i.e. a mixture of

Jacobean and Elizabethan, by the local architect brothers Robert and John Goodacre. The late 14th century chapel retains much of its original character, despite restoration in 1876 by Thomas Nevinson, a Leicester architect, who imported some fixtures and fittings from other establishments, including a two-light thirteenth century stone window for the vestry from an old building at Ashby Folville.

The chapel, which was reopened by the Bishop of Peterborough in October 1904, retains its four lancet east window, with 1905 coloured glass by Christopher Whall depicting archangels, and an alabaster monument, possibly to Mary Hervey who was a member of Henry IV's household. The 14th century encaustic tiled floor exhibits coats of arms, heraldry, animals and text.

(Photograph: The Trinity Hospital,
Leicester, S.H. Skillington)

The residents of the almshouse were relocated in new accommodation designed by HLM Architects of Sheffield and built by Wimpey Construction Ltd., adjacent to the river in 1995. The sale of the old buildings in the Newarke (New Work) to De Montfort University was accomplished using the seal of 1615 with its Latin inscription 'SIGIL HOSPITALIS SCTAE TRINITATIS IN NOVO OPERE LEIC' (Seal of the Hospital of the Holy Trinity in the New Work of Leicester). The Trinity Building now accommodates the senior management of the university in the twentieth century section of the building. The original chapel is used for special events including concerts and ceremonial occasions. The large 61 gallon cooking pot known as 'The Duke of Lancaster's Porridge (Pottage) Pot' and other artefacts formerly in the old hospital are now located in the new Trinity Hospital building.

Duke of Lancaster's Porridge (Pottage) Pot, now located in the new Trinity Hospital. (Photograph: Leicester's Royal Foundation – The Hospital of the Holy Trinity, T.Y. Cocks)

Gardens to the rear of Trinity House
(Photograph: De Montfort University)

Stone for the rebuilding of the
Trinity Hospital in 1901

Plaque detailing the history of the
Trinity Hospital

Interior of Trinity House

Alabaster Monument – c.1400, possibly Mary Hervey, wife of William Hervey.
(Photograph: De Montfort University)

Dame Mary Hervey in 1406 provided an endowment for the hospital of five pence per year to each of the almspeople on the anniversary of her death.

Cottages in The Newarke

Adjacent to the chapel of the Trinity Hospital is a terrace of four cottages (15, 17, 19 and 21 The Newarke) which was built as two joined up pairs in 1870. The Victorian brickwork detailing and barge boards on the right hand pair being more decorative than on the other pair. The university occupies number 17 White Rose Cottage and number 19. Number 15 was originally occupied by the Clerk of St Mary's Church.

Deacon's Workshop (below left);
Deacon's Workshop Interior (below)

To the rear of number 21, adjacent to the Turret Gateway in Castle View, is the early 18th century red brick and slate, grade II Listed 'Deacon's Workshop'. The building was probably built as a store, but it was subsequently used as a museum reconstruction of Samuel Deacon (1746-1816), the clockmaker's workshop. The Deacons were a well-known family of Leicestershire clockmakers, which continued through several generations until 1951. The clockface formerly on one gable, but now located in the Newarke Houses Museum, is inscribed Deacon 1771. In 2004 the University of Leicester Archaeological Services discovered, adjacent to its foundations, evidence of human burials which predate the building.

Chantry Building

The Chantry Building, now the Square Mile Hub, was formerly St Mary's Vicarage and early pictures illustrate it as a three storey building. However, most of the building was demolished in 1947, leaving only the single storey seen today. This listed building has now been stabilised and is the base for the university's Square Mile programme which gives students volunteering opportunities within the local community. The project encourages the innovative use of skills and expertise to create positive change within the city of Leicester.

An illustration of the construction of the adjacent Portland Shoe Factory in 1889, shows the rear of the original three-storey building, whilst the photograph prior to 1947 shows the original front façade. The street frontage is now The Gateway, however when built, the location was called Asylum Street, because of the female asylum on the corner with The Newarke opposite Trinity House. Asylum Street was renamed Gateway Street in the 1960s and more recently changed through the influence of the University to The Gateway. The Chantry building was used as a store by the adjacent Portland Shoe factory for much of the twentieth century.

Recent archaeological work by University of Leicester Archaeological Services suggests that the building was the 14th century residence of the dean or one of the canons associated with the 14th Collegiate Church of St Mary, of which two arches remain in the basement of the Hawthorn Building. From the 17th century, the vicars of St Mary de Castro (literally castle) lived here and later it became a school.

Chantry Building prior to 1947
(Photograph: Castle Park – A Souvenir Guide, Leicester County Council. Reproduced by permission of the Record Office for Leicestershire, Leicester and Rutland)

Rear of the Chantry Building in 1889
(Photograph: Reproduced by permission of the Record Office for Leicestershire, Leicester and Rutland)

Chancellor's House

The Chancellor's House, Number 1 Richmond Street, with accommodation for the vice-chancellor and a corporate hospitality suite, was previously part of the Gateway Sixth Form College, which vacated the building in 2009, when the college moved to Hamilton. The elegant 1772 Georgian residence facing Magazine Square, bears the elusive initials W.M. This residence had been variously occupied in the 19th century by Dr John Barclay (medical officer of health), Lord Viscount Ingestre and John Stockdale Hardy. In 1891 the house became St Mary Magdalene's Refuge for Fallen Women – a charity run by Anglican Nuns to restore fallen women under maternal influence, and to train them in moral and industrial habits for domestic or other service. The building was sold to Leicester Corporation in 1923 for £4,500.

The well-proportioned house is characterised by a typical Georgian Doric column and pediment doorway with a semi-circular fanlight over the panelled door. Sash timber windows of standard-sized panes are set below brick vousoir arches with featured keystones. The modilion cornice partially obscures the slated hipped roof. Originally, the house extended along the former Fairfax Street with various outbuildings, stables and coach-

Georgian doorway

Rainwater head

Interior

houses. Internally the house retains some of its original features including fireplaces. The basement was converted into a crypt in 1963 following a gift of £500 by Alderman C.R.Keene.

De Montfort University refurbished the building to a high standard, restoring the original architectural character and detailing, whilst incorporating technological solutions including IT, a building management system and energy efficient fittings.

Crypt wall detail

Heritage House

The development of Heritage House on the corner of Southgate Street and Castle Street offers a good illustration of the growth of a successful Leicester hosiery business at the turn of the nineteenth century. A company leaflet claims that the S.D. Stretton and Sons' business was founded in 1796, but the first record of their location at 59½ Southgate Street appears in 1870. By 1875, Stephen Dudgeon Stretton (1820-1901) had expanded his activity as Stretton & Hutchinson Hosiery Manufacturers and occupied 61 Southgate Street as his warehouse.

A further warehouse designed by the architect James Frank Smith was developed behind the Southgate Street building in 1885, and this was quickly followed in 1892 by the addition of a factory unit in Castle Street – now the middle portion of that elevation. The projecting red brick piers give a strong vertical emphasis to the industrial façade. At this time the corner of Southgate Street and Castle Street was occupied

by three-storey dwellings and shops, but these were replaced in 1901 by the current corner block, designed by Keites & Fosbrooke architects. The Classical style, incorporating stone columns with ionic capitals, stone banding and decorative windows, acted as a strong visual statement to reflect the growing success of the business. The third window on the Castle Street elevation was originally the dray entrance.

Subsequently in 1914, Keites, Fosbrooke & Bedingfield designed the section of the building down Castle Street to the boundary with the St. Mary de Castro churchyard. This section includes the Arts and Crafts style Grade II red brick listed tower with its chateau-style roof, pinnacles and trefoil-headed windows, also the highly decorative carved stone entrance.

After the closure of Stretton Knitwear in 1989, the building was converted into offices, to design work by the Douglas Smith Stimson Partnership, for the Alliance & Leicester Building

Society. It was subsequently acquired from Santander by the University in 2013 for teaching accommodation and IT services.

The tower

Castle Street façade

Clephan Building

The Clephan Building, location for humanities within the Faculty of Arts, Design and Humanities and part of the Faculty of Technology, is located on Oxford Street. The building was built over a period of thirty years, originally as a hosiery factory and warehouse for I. & R. Morley Ltd. The building, square C-shaped in plan, encloses a courtyard incorporating the Music Technology Innovation studio. The brick boiler house chimney was demolished during refurbishment and reorientation of the building in 1993.

The first phase of construction in 1885 as a warehouse/factory, was the four-storey and basement north-west wing, 25 Oxford Street, which included the one remaining arched street access and the removed boiler-house chimney, which had been located near to the current main entrance. The building was designed in February 1884 by the well-known Leicester Architect, Stockdale Harrison for the builder Harry Bland. The first extension, which was to the rear of the first phase, was designed in 1888 by H. Bland to a lower roof line. The builder, H. Bland, occupied 27 Oxford Street, on which the later Clephan Building extensions were built, extended his own house on that site in 1891; he had previously moved from Castle Street in 1878.

The grand brick, stone and decorative faience Oxford Street façade was designed by Keites & Fosbrooke, architects and surveyors of Leicester as the major extension of 1901. Internal exposed cast iron columns and external window cills show minor variation from the first phase of construction. This phase of construction was the most opulent reflecting the success of the company and the wealth of the

Cast iron column

owners. The 'Queen Anne Style' terracotta panels are of sunflowers, which were popular motifs at that time. The status of the building is accentuated on the Oxford Street façade by the second and third floor oriel windows surmounted by columns to a raised roof.

The last major development was to the corner of Oxford Street and the south-east wing along Bonners Lane. This phase, designed by Keites, Fosbrooke and Bedingfield of Market Street, Leicester in 1914, illustrates the ability of early twentieth century architects to make a strong visual statement in turning corners. The detailing of

the doorway particularly reflects 1913-14 contemporary architectural style. During the first phases of construction the masonry was up to 820mm thick, with cast iron columns and large timber beams giving open machinery space, under a timber and slate roof. The Bonners Lane section is built with steel in conjunction with brick and timber reflecting changing forms of construction. From 1916 onwards the building was shared by I. & R. Morley and S. Rowsell & Co. the boot and shoe manufacturer. The factories eventually closed and the building was finally sold to the local education authority in 1967.

Faience detail

(Photograph: De Montfort University)

(Photograph: De Montfort University)

The building was converted to use for higher education in 1970. Ownership was transferred from Leicester City Council to Leicestershire County Council in 1974. The building was upgraded with new entrance canopies by Jonathan Smith in 1993 and subsequently refurbished by Church Lukas of Nottingham for the Faculties of Arts, Design & Humanities and Technology in 2000, with new lifts, windows, and an additional fire escape. The building is named after the art collector and philanthropist Mr Edwin Clephan (1817-1906) who was the first chairman of the School of Art Sub-committee.

The Music Technology Innovation studio in the courtyard was originally built as the Design Technology Unit (DTU on the door) for the School of Architecture. It was designed by Gil Lewis and built by Stuart Berry with donated materials acquired by Arthur Lyons. The unit was officially opened on 19 May 1987 by Sir John Banham as Director General of the CBI. The flat canopy roof had been originally installed as part of the 1970 boiler house construction, to provide a covered area for students of architecture and surveying to experience practical building skills, such as bricklaying, carpentry and tiling.

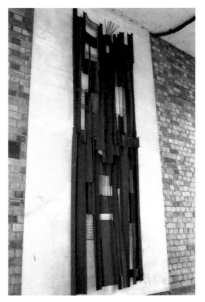

Untitled sculpture by George Pickard, 1970 (Photograph: De Montfort University)

Within the original Clephan archway is an untitled mild steel wall sculpture by George Pickard. The 1970 work of art was originally located in the reception area of Oakland Elevators, Oadby, but was removed in 1996, and donated to De Montfort University.

Below: Farmer & his Wife, Yoma Sasburgh, 1992

Portland Building

The Portland Building was built in 1889 for the Portland Shoe Company which had been founded in 1872 by Thomas Roberts. The street at that time was Asylum Street, but was renamed Gateway Street and subsequently The Gateway. The drawings for the proposed factory/warehouse by the architect Edgar Burgess dated November 1888 and for the chimney in 1889, show a much grander façade in classical style with a parapet, than is seen today. This was due to the disastrous fire of 1908 which completely gutted the building requiring the factory to be rebuilt in 1909 to its present form.

Plans submitted to the Borough Council, 1888
(Drawing: Reproduced by permission of the Record Office for Leicestershire, Leicester and Rutland)

Portland Shoes factory after the fire, 1908
(Photograph: Reproduced by permission of the Record Office for Leicestershire, Leicester and Rutland)

The factory was extended in 1914 and 1921. The oldest part includes the forty foot frontage along Asylum Street, now The Gateway, with two oriel windows at first floor level and the small dormer windows over the entrance section. The chimney of 1889 has been removed. The later addition into Goswell Street, now Newarke Close, features an interesting skyline with the brick piers projecting above the parapet. The company ceased trading in 1989, after celebrating its centenary in 1972 with the business managed successively by five generations of the founder's family.

Prior to building the Portland factory, Thomas Roberts travelled to America to study the latest technologies to bring these ideas back to England for incorporation into the new building in The Newarke. At the time of the company centenary in 1972, the management was confident that the business would operate for a further hundred years! Photographs of the office and the sample room with stock lines, reflect the quality of the brand name, Portland Shoes, worn by nobility and even British Airways hostesses in 1952.

Portland Shoes Office
(Photograph: Reproduced by
permission of the Record Office
for Leicestershire, Leicester
and Rutland)

Portland Shoes Sample Room
(Photograph: Reproduced by
permission of the Record Office
for Leicestershire, Leicester
and Rutland)

Portland Shoes Factory
before the fire of 1908
(Photograph: Reproduced by
permission of the Record Office
for Leicestershire, Leicester
and Rutland)

The bird's eye sketch for a shoe box label shows a greatly expanded building.

Portland Shoe Works printed on shoe boxes (Photograph: Castle Park – A Souvenir Guide, Leicester County Council. Reproduced by permission of the Record Office for Leicestershire, Leicester and Rutland)

Eaves detail

The factory, now as the Portland Building of the University, occupies the site of 'the New College of Annunciation of Our Lady in the Newarke'. During excavations for the foundations and basement of the building a silvered spur and cannon ball were found with a skeleton of a horse and two men, possibly from the siege of Leicester by King Charles.

The building was purchased by the University in 1991 and converted for educational use. It currently offers classroom accommodation together with university administrative and educational support facilities. The red brick building is characterised by its strong Italianate cornice and the decorative carved stone entrance doorway with Ionic columns. These are surmounted on the architrave by crouching rather pensive draped female figures against foliage backgrounds and bent below the open segmental pediment. The figures each rest their heads upon a raised hand, although their poses differ. The original brass plaques relating to Portland Shoes have been removed from either side of the double doors, but the iron railings are original.

The single storey building originally behind the Portland Building, which for a brief period was the University Chaplaincy, had originally been the canteen for the Portland Shoe Factory. This building was demolished for the construction of the Newarke Point Hall of Residence.

In 1921, C. Roberts of Portland Shoes owned 'Villiers House' in Oadby designed by T. Henry Bowell as his private residence. This is now the Gilbert Murray Hall of the University of Leicester.

It is of interest that De Montfort University, based in Leicester with its heritage of hosiery and footwear manufacture, is one of only three university institutions in England offering degree programmes in footwear design.

Carved stone entrance detail
(Photograph: De Montfort University)

Hawthorn Building

The Hawthorn Building, which houses a significant section of the Health and Life Sciences Faculty, is square in plan. The front wing was built in 1897 as the School of Art and Technical School in orange red Leicester brick with Portland stone window surrounds, moulded string courses and banding. The façade is articulated to emphasise the entrance and the corners. The arched front entrance, decorated with stone cartouches and approached by steps and ornate iron gates, is surmounted by a bracketed cornice ending in shell motifs. The building was designed by Messrs Everard and Pick whose practice continues in Leicester under the title Pick Everard. The builders were Messrs T. & H. Herbert. The foundation stone was laid on 30 March 1896 by the Chairman of the Committee and the Mayor, and the building was officially opened on 5 October 1897 by the Rt Hon. and Rt Rev. Mandell Creighton who was the Bishop of London at that time. The building is named after the first Head Master of the technical school, Mr J.H. Hawthorn BA. The first extension, the south wing, was completed in similar architectural style by T. Herbert in 1909.

Original Plans for the Hawthorn Building

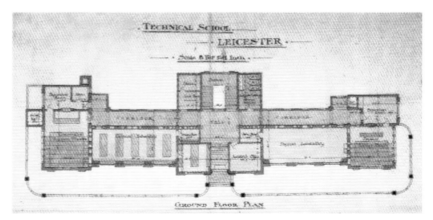

Foundation Stone, 1896

Shoes Factory, fortunately show The Newarke and Asylum Street two-storey façades to the old asylum with their arched windows.

By 1887, the nearby St Mary's Magdalene's 'Refuge and Friendless Girls Home' also described as the 'Refuge and Night Shelter for Fallen Women' had been established under the Superioress Sister Mary Louisa. It was located on the corner of Richmond Street, (now the Chancellor's House) in the former home of the physician, Dr John Barclay, where The Newarke previously curved round in front of the current Hawthorn Building.

In 1927, Her Grace, The Duchess of Atholl laid the foundation stone for the west wing, which was completed in 1928, by which time the institution was renamed the Leicester Colleges of Art & Technology.

The north-west corner of the Hawthorn Building stands on the site of the former asylum, which gave its name to Asylum Street, now The Gateway. The asylum, commenced in 1800 and clearly indicated on the 1828 map of Leicester, was established to support sixteen poor girls who entered at the age of thirteen under the supervision of a matron. They stayed for three years and were trained for 'domestic servitude'. The asylum later became the 'Female Asylum and Orphanage' and was finally closed soon after 1925 for the site to be redeveloped for the Leicester Colleges. The photographs, taken around 1889, at the time of the development of the new Portland

The Asylum Entrance on the right of The Newarke (Photograph: Reproduced by permission of the Record Office for Leicestershire, Leicester and Rutland)

Clearly The Newarke was an area of Leicester, particularly associated with support to poorer members of the community. It is certainly coincidental that the original buildings, Hawthorn and Fielding Johnson, of De Montfort University and the University of Leicester respectively, are both associated with asylums, although differing significantly in size and function.

In 1930 the College was recognised for the External Degree in Pharmacy of London University, and by 1934 London University recognised the College as suitable for preparing students for the External Degree in Engineering. The fourth phase of construction was the north

The Asylum on the left
of Asylum Street
(Photograph: Reproduced by
permission of the Record Office for
Leicestershire, Leicester and Rutland)

Foundation Stone for the
West Wing, 1927

wing facing Trinity House. This was completed in 1938-39 with large steel framed windows in the prevalent 1930s Art Deco style.

The decoration includes cinquefoils and three relief panels in limestone attributed to Percy Brown. The coat of arms over the doorway is dated 1937. The two pendant high relief sculptures form a pair. It is suggested that the left sculpture represents Venus rising from the waves with a fish to her left elbow and stars above her head. The right sculpture may represent Adonis, the object of Venus's love. He is depicted as the young hunter with his bow, looking left towards a bird.

North Wing, 1939

Cinquefoil decoration

'Venus rising from the waves'

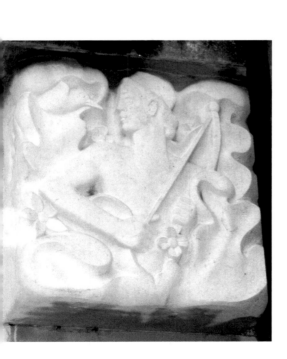

'Adonis, the young hunter'

The 1937 doors to the north façade are delightfully embellished with low relief copper panels by Percy Brown depicting the tools of art, crafts, science and technology. Percy Brown was Lecturer in Sculpture at the Leicester College of Art from 1935 to 1946.

Low relief copper panels
by Percy Brown, 1937

(Photograph: De Montfort University)

This masonry is all that remains of the Collegiate Church of the Annunciation of Our Lady of the Newarke at Leicester, which was founded in 1354 by Henry Plantagenet, First Duke of Lancaster and Fourth Lancastrian Earl of Leicester. The masonry was removed from its site during the extension of the Colleges of Art and Technology and was replaced in its original position in October 1937.

* * *

Collegiate Church of the Annunciation
of Our Lady of The Newarke

Crypt of the Collegiate Church
of the Annunciation of
Our Lady of the Newarke

Within the basement of the north wing are the ruins of the Collegiate Church of the Annunciation of our Lady of the Newarke at Leicester, founded in 1354 by Henry Plantagenet. These remains, which formed part of the crypt, were in the cellar of an old house which was demolished in 1931 for the extension of the College. They were then restored in 1937 and are now preserved as the centrepiece of the University Heritage Centre which illustrates the history and achievements of the university within the context of historic Leicester.

Street lamps in The Newarke

The Church of the Annunciation was destroyed in the Reformation, but it is believed that battle-scarred body of Richard III was laid out there on public view for two days after his defeat by Henry Tudor at the battle of Bosworth Field in 1485. Richard III was then buried in Grey Friars monastery, near to the present cathedral where his bones were subsequently re-interred in March 2015.

The building is located in a historic part of the city, illustrated by the 'Whipping Toms' notice on the posts associated with the decorative front railings. Two 1937 lamp posts define the north entrance to the building, but the original square section lamps have been replaced by poor replicas. The mature plane tree gives scale to Hawthorn Square enclosed by the modern Hugh Aston Building and the Georgian Chancellor's House.

THE WHIPPING TOMS

ON THIS SPOT STOOD THE WHIPPING TOMS, WHO, ON SHROVE TUESDAY, IN ACCORDANCE WITH THE ANCIENT CUSTOM, ARMED THEMSELVES WITH WAGON WHIPS AND FLOGGED ANYONE WHO ENTERED THE PRECINCTS OF THE NEWARKE. THE SPORT WAS ABOLISHED BY ACT OF PARLIAMENT IN 1846.

The Whipping Toms

Old Castle Inn - 12 Castle View

The present building 12 Castle View, formally known as the 'Old Castle Inn' was built in 1898 to plans by W. Beaumont-Smith, County Surveyor. The random rubble building in Gothic Revival style is characterised by stone quoins, mock timber framing and dominant bargeboards. The large jettied front window and two oriel bays give individuality to the built form.

The site had previously been occupied by an earlier 'Old Castle Inn', but this was demolished together with the adjoining terraced house which was removed to give the current side gate access. The rebuilt tavern, considerably deeper in plan, was double the size of the earlier building. The pub finally closed in the 1970s and was then used intermittently by the university as office space.

The first tavern on the site, dating back to 1815, was known as the 'Castle Bowling Green' with Thomas Martin as landlord. Subsequently the pub became known variously as the 'Castle Inn' and the 'Old Castle Inn', with the latter name remaining after the rebuild until the mid-1970s.

(Photograph: Reproduced by permission of the Record Office for Leicestershire, Leicester and Rutland)

The Venue@DMU

The Venue@DMU, a multipurpose conference and events centre for exhibitions, examinations, degree and matriculation ceremonies, is a redevelopment of the former early twentieth century John Sandford Sports Centre. The refurbished timber-clad building has foldaway 'Bleacher' seating and can be subdivided by folding partitions into three smaller spaces. The £3.7m conversion designed by CPMG Architects and constructed by Stepnell Ltd., Building and Civil Engineering Contractors, was officially opened in September 2015 by the Vice-Chancellor Dominic Shellard in association with members of the student body.

The original building, commissioned by the Boulevard Rink Company Limited and designed by William M. Cowdell in 1909 was specifically built for roller skating. The brick building is characterised by the innovative wooden roof structure comprising Anderson's Patent Belfast Trusses, which are retained although largely obscured by the necessary modern lighting systems.

Installation of the Chancellor of the University Baroness Doreen Lawrence of Clarendon MBE in The Venue@DMU
(Photograph: De Montfort University)

Former and new interior

By the 1930s, the building had become a popular venue for boxing contests. Sport was suspended during the Second World War, when the building was used for the production of spitfire aircraft wings due to its strategic location adjacent to the Great Central Railway. After the war the building was owned by the Education Committee and in 1947 it was taken over by the former Leicester College of Art & Design. The John Sandford Sports Centre offered gymnasium facilities with a fitness suite, sauna and sun beds together with a hall for indoor football, basketball, badminton and squash.

John Sandford, a former national swimmer and basketball player for England, was Head of Physical Education at Leicester Polytechnic and its previous constituent colleges from 1952 to his sudden death in 1974 when the sports building was named in his memory. John Sandford as a keen sportsman set up a wide range of activities including basketball, badminton, canoeing and swimming for the college students.

John Whitehead Building

The John Whitehead building was designed by Henry Neal for Henry Herbert and Sons, the local builders. It was constructed in 1909 as a factory for '170 hands'. The original building of three storeys and a basement had a fifty foot frontage and was orientated at right angles to Newarke Street. By 1911, the building was occupied by the blouse manufacturer William Baker. In 1912, he extended the building by opening up the roof space as a store, which required the insertion of additional cast iron columns to the third floor level. In 1914, Tait and Herbert Architects drew up plans for the larger adjacent building along Newarke Street. The new building, of brick steel and timber construction, with four storeys and a basement was completed in 1915. Henry Herbert & Sons maintained a builders yard

in this vicinity, at least until 1916. By 1928, William Baker was listed in local registers as a hosiery, rather than blouse manufacturer. The original red brick William Baker Building and the adjacent three and four storey properties, including the three storey Wildt & Co. factory (hosiery machine builders) of 1907, now the 'Soar Point' public house towards the canal, form an appropriate townscape leading down to the 1898 'Gothic Revival' Newarke Bridge. This spans the 'Mile Straight' of the river Soar canal which had been 'cut' in 1889. The triangular space between the Chantry House and the original William Baker Building was only occupied around 1917 by minor sheds and outhouses for the William Baker factory and currently remains unbuilt.

It is interesting to note that Albert Herbert was trained in the Leicester School of Art (now De Montfort University School of Architecture) and initially was articled to James Tait of Friar Lane, Leicester.

After it had become vacant, the William Baker Building was purchased by the University in 2007 for conversion into offices. It was temporarily named as 12 The Newarke until it was officially renamed the John Whitehead Building to commemorate the former Polytechnic Chairman of Governors and University Pro-Chancellor who died in March 2008. John Whitehead was Deputy Lord Lieutenant and High Sheriff of Leicester and a Justice of the Peace. The building is currently occupied by the university administration.

Rear of the John Whitehead Building
(Photograph:
De Montfort University)

Estate Development Building

The Estate Development Building is part of the former Gateway College complex. In 1976 the Gateway School became the Gateway Sixth Form College, and the following year it acquired the 1930 Richmond House which had been the City's Educational Health Clinic, and this rounded off the college's campus bounded by Mill Lane, Gateway Street (formerly Asylum Street) and Richmond Street. In 1995 the dental service buildings along Richmond Street were demolished to make way for the library, opened the following year as the Frazer Building, named after Dr H. Frazer the Gateway School's headmaster from 1952 to 1971.

The Estate Development Building therefore comprises a refurbished part of the original Health Clinic buildings together with the 1996 Gateway Sixth Form College Library.

Since its acquisition in 2009, De Montfort University has refurbished the buildings to provide a flexible and compliant high-quality office environment for its Estates' Directorate.

Estate Development Building

Health Clinic (Photograph: Gateway Sixth Form College)

Estate Development Building – The former Gateway Sixth Form College Library

Philip Tasker Building

The former Fairfax Street elevation

The Philip Tasker Building was formerly the main building of the Gateway College. It is currently occupied by the Leicester International Pathway College and the university directorate of student services.

The Gateway Boys' School was founded in 1928 as a development from the colleges of Art and Technology. It occupied, until 1939, Skeffington House which now forms part of the Newarke Houses Museum. When purchased by the City Council in 1923, it had been intended that the Georgian house, now the Chancellor's House, would be used for the City's Educational Offices, however this proved to be unsatisfactory. So when in 1928 plans were made to establish a Gateway Girls' School, the building was extended along Fairfax Street to a design by George Nott, who was the Head of the School of Architecture in the Art School. George Nott also designed Bredon House at Oadby, now owned by the University of Leicester. The 1931 extensions sensitively continued the style of the Georgian façade with featured keystone windows, cornice and matching brickwork. The centrepiece of this major development was a decorative plaque with the City of Leicester arms and motto, framed by two square-sectioned pillars surmounted by urns. The Gateway Girls School moved into the building in 1932. However, the economic depression of the 30s and subsequent government spending cuts led in 1939 to the move by the Gateway Girls School, away from this site to Imperial Avenue, leaving

Leicester Coat of Arms

the buildings available for the boys' school. Girls were eventually admitted to the Gateway School in 1976. The Fairfax Street building originally had a roof top yard to which prefabs were added in 1946 to give extra accommodation. These were renovated in the mid-1970s and eventually replaced in the 1990s by the current permanent accommodation featuring an over-sailing roof and decorative pediment. A science lecture theatre was built between the two wings of the building in 1958. The school became the Gateway Sixth Form College in 1976 and they vacated the building on their move to Hamilton in 2009.

The Philip Tasker Building with 1946 'prefabs' on the rooftop (Photograph: History of Gateway School 1928-1978)

The building is named after Philip Tasker who was Vice-Chancellor of the university from 1999 to 2010.

Typical Classroom (Photograph: Gateway School Prospectus 1939)

Art Factory, Mill Studios and The Greenhouse

Art Factory

The Art Factory, Mill Studios and The Greenhouse were built in the 1960s as extensions to the Gateway School. At that time the Gateway School had decided to remain on its Leicester site (now part of the University) and extend to the southwest over Fairfax Street, as the sub-standard terraced housing in that area was being demolished. Phase I of this development was the two-storey Art Factory on Mill Lane, which was constructed using the CLASP (Consortium of Local Authorities Special Programme) system to a design by the City Architects Department at a cost of £60,000. The construction was not without problems, as after the steelwork had been erected, it had to be removed to reinforce the five-inch concrete raft. The system required the steel frame to be fitted onto steel dowels embedded in the concrete raft. The prefabricated walls of concrete and timber were them hung and clamped onto the framework. The building was finally occupied in 1962, but was criticised at the time as the lightweight construction permitted the building to move gently in the wind.

Phase II of the development, the three-storey building along Richmond Street, was completed in 1966 at a cost of £200,000.

Mill Studios - The Gateway

It is anticipated that in the medium term the Mill Studios and Art Factory may be removed to create the open space link between Hawthorn Square and the landscaped Mill Lane. The Greenhouse in Richmond Street is currently the third learning zone within the University, in addition to those in the Kimberlin library and the Eric Wood building.

Mill Studios - Mill Lane

The Greenhouse – Richmond Street

Gateway House

Gateway House, base for the School of Computer Science and Informatics within the Faculty of Technology, and some student services, is located on The Gateway between Deacon Street and Gosling Street. The building was built by Wheatcroft (Houses) Ltd. as a speculative 'multiple warehouse' block in 1965 for Leicester City Council, offering showrooms and lettable space for occupancy by small industrial units and offices. It was designed by Barton Everitt and Calow of London Road Leicester in 1964. The University leased the building in 1990, and gradually took up occupancy of more of the accommodation as the various private companies departed. The City Council engaged with the University over the ownership of the building which was finally transferred in 2006.

The concrete-frame building is cruciform in plan, although this is not apparent from any street view. The rather bland brick and panel façades were enhanced in 1989 by the addition of a significant pattern of chevron-shaped sun-shades, designed by Cathy Stewart of Peake, Short and Partners. Also decorative panels at roof and street level were added. However, the sun-shades were removed during further major refurbishment in 2007 which involved replacement of the substandard windows.

Sun-shades – now removed
(Photograph: 'The Quality of Leicester',
Leicester City Council)

When taken over by the University a number of beehives were found on the flat roof, and inside, assorted bee-keeping equipment and football trophies were discovered.

Internally the entrance foyer and system of lifts have been upgraded to ease previous circulation difficulties associated with moving large numbers of students, as opposed to small numbers of visitors to commercial organisations.

Decorative panel details

(Photograph: De Montfort University)

Edith Murphy House

Edith Murphy House, formerly Bosworth House, was completed in 1974 as a speculative office block. It was designed by Grinling and Crisp of London, with concrete structural calculations by Bison. It was built by Cubit for Metropolitan Estate & Property Corporation as a concrete and glass structure, typical of many 1970s speculative office buildings. The massing consists of a combination of nine, five and four storeys, which relates more to the adjacent commercial buildings in Southgates, rather than the Castle Conservation Area of the Newarke Houses Museum and St Mary de Castro Church. Initially the University occupied just two floors but gradually took over the whole building and the car parking area as various leases became available. Bosworth House was occupied by the Leicester Business School within the Faculty of Business and Law until their new accommodation in the Hugh Aston Building became available.

The building was totally refurbished in 2011 by JSP Architecture and Baggaley Construction to accommodate part of the Faculty of Health and Life Sciences including the School of Nursing and Midwifery, which had been moved from its Charles Frears Campus, to consolidate all activities onto the one university site.

The £8 million refurbishment included the construction of a new tower to enhance vertical circulation, leading from a new entrance off Magazine Square. Additionally all windows,

Edith Murphy House

Tree detail

mechanical, electrical and water systems were replaced to ensure maximum energy and environmental efficiency.

The refurbished building, which features a decorative tree design on the glazed tower, is named after the philanthropist, Edith Murphy, whose many donations included £400,000 for the development of an artificial pancreas currently being produced at the university. The building was officially opened by Dr Dame Clare Bertschinger in October 2011. Dame Bertschinger is the holder of many awards including the Florence Nightingale Medal, the Woman of the Year Window to the World Award and the International Human Rights and Nursing Award. She was appointed Dame Commander of the British Empire in the 2010 New Year Honours List, and an honorary doctorate of science from De Montfort University in 2009.

The form Bosworth Hou

Eric Wood Building

The Eric Wood university administrative building was formally opened by Mr R.E. Wood CBE on 15 October 1975. The building was named after Eric Wood who had been the Principal of the Leicester College of Technology from 1953 to 1969, and the first Director of Leicester Polytechnic from 1969 to 1973.

The building was designed by the Leicester City Architects under the leadership of Mr K.J. King (City Architect) together with Leicestershire County Architects under the leadership of Mr T. Locke (County Architect). The building of three floors, is constructed of a concrete frame, with concrete upper floors. The external walls are of hard smooth red semi-engineering facing bricks, which feature brick 'specials' in the detailing of plinths, quoins and parapets. The external brickwork is carried through into some of the internal spaces, to create contrast between the hard wall surfaces and the softer timber finishes and furnishings.

The building was designed to house the expanding administrative services which had previously been distributed in various buildings, and to create meeting rooms for the various Polytechnic committees. However, with the expansion of the University, the senior management were relocated to Trinity House and other university administration moved into the refurbished John Whitehead Building. This latter relocation has enabled the core university 'Learning Zone' to be extended into the ground floor of the

Eric Wood building. It is anticipated that eventually the whole Eric Wood building will be transferred from administration to student learning, further extending the library facilities.

Learning zone entrance

Queen's Building

The Queen's Building, part of the Faculty of Technology, is certainly the most well-known of De Montfort University's buildings. It was designed by Alan Short and Brian Ford of Peake Short & Partners. Feasibility studies focussed on developing a methodology to bring together environmental issues with academic and financial considerations. A major factor was to design a high technology building with appropriate comfort levels, in which large quantities of heat were generated from occupants, computers and other machinery, but without mechanical ventilation. The design brief required traditional construction to support the local construction industry, but equally demanded innovation and environmental sensitivity to challenge current and emergent design criteria. A high priority for the architectural team was to limit building energy consumption to the minimum possible, by eliminating air conditioning and using natural stack and cross ventilation. Natural lighting was to be available to all occupants of the building.

The building is constructed of load-bearing polychromatic brickwork; externally with coral red brick enhanced with silver buff and cadmium red, and internally in the concourse with warm yellow calcium silicate brick banded with delicate combinations of ivory, white, cinnamon, green and midnight blue. Smaller spaces are finished in fairfaced blockwork but with some decorative brick banding. The wide insulation-filled cavity brickwork

acts as a large thermal mass, reducing temperature fluctuations. Cruciform steelwork sections are used internally to support the brick stack ventilation columns within the concourse. The mainly pitched roof structure is a combination of steel ridge trusses and timber rafters.

In more detail, the building consists of a central core with the main lecture theatre facilities and three wings for the laboratories. The front two wings partially enclose the shady entrance courtyard, which acts as a sump of cool air for the internal spaces. In the central core, the auditoria are ventilated through sound baffled brickwork vents and exhausted through the tall stacks. Smaller laboratory and teaching spaces have low-level opening windows and high-level vents for natural ventilation. Daylight

penetrates into the central atrium through roof lights and into top storey studio space through large gable windows.

The two front wings are cross ventilated, and naturally light, but direct sunlight is controlled by light shelves which eliminate direct sunlight by reflecting it onto ceilings to produce a more even level of natural lighting. The large laboratory space is ventilated through low level perforated brick buttresses and exhausted through the gable roof lights which admit appropriate levels of natural lighting. Direct sunlight penetration is prevented by deep eaves details.

Whilst initially the building raised questions of its design within context, it is now generally accepted as a strong visual statement within the De Montfort University campus.

Interior atrium
(Photograph: De Montfort University)

Exterior brickwork detailing

Interior brickwork details

The Queen's Building is occupied by the School of Engineering and Sustainable Development within the Faculty of Technology also, appropriately, the Institute for Sustainable Energy and Development which carries out a broad range of research into sustainable building and renewable energy.

The Queen's Building has won several architectural awards including the RIBA Education Building of the Year, 1995; Quality in Brickwork Award 1994; Civic Trust Commendation, 1995 and The Independent Newspaper 'Green Building of the Year', 1995. The building created a stylistic precedent which was soon followed in 2000 by the Short & Associates deep plan, Library and Learning Resource Centre for Coventry University, which also relied heavily on natural stack ventilation.

The cedar-shingle clad bridge between the Kimberlin Library and the Queen's Building was incorporated into the scheme to permit the new building to be VAT zero rated, as an extension to an existing building, under the regulations operative at the time.

The Lanchester Library of Coventry University - Short & Associates, 2000

Bridge linking the Queen's Building to the Kimberlin Library

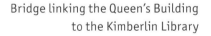

The Official Opening by Her Majesty The Queen (Photograph: Lionel Grech)

Her Majesty The Queen with Vice-Chancellor Professor Kenneth Barker and the Queen's Building Architects, Alan Short and Brian Ford (Photograph: Lionel Grech)

Professor Kenneth Barker by
Sean Henry, 1999

Over the entrance to the Queen's Building is a bronze statue of Professor Kenneth Barker who was Vice-Chancellor from 1987 to 1999.

The foundation stone was laid by HRH The Duke of Gloucester and the building was completed in 1993. It was officially opened by Her Majesty The Queen on 9 December 1993, who granted the University permission to name the building the 'Queen's Building'.

Her Majesty The Queen's official tour
(Photograph: Lionel Grech)

Innovation Centre

The Innovation Centre was opened in 1995 on the corner of Oxford Street and Bonners Lane. During excavations for the building by the University of Leicester Archaeological Services, the remains of a Saxon House, circa 600 AD, the first in Leicester, were discovered on the site. The sunken building featured post and stake holes, pottery fragments and a near complete double-sided bone comb. A second sunken building, presumed to be part of the same settlement, was subsequently discovered on the other side of Oxford Street.

(Photograph: De Montfort University)

The Innovation Centre was built through a City Challenge partnership between Leicester City and De Montfort University under the Training and Technology Transfer (TTT) scheme. It is the location for spin-off industries arising from university research and development projects. The building designed by Douglas Smith Stimson Partnership is leased by the University. The banded brickwork shows some accidental colouring effects associated with variation of colour between different packs of bricks not appropriately randomised on site.

(Photograph: De Montfort University)

Faculty of Technology – Bede Island

The Faculty of Technology – Bede Island building was formerly the Leicester Business School Graduate Centre. It is on the island formed between the two branches of the River Soar. The main canal branch flows near to the University campus along the 'Straight Mile'. Originally, Bede Island was the site of three scrap recycling businesses; Frank Berry, Vic Berry and A.E. Piggott which were closed down after a serious fire. The site was decontaminated through an urban regeneration initiative 'City Challenge' by Leicester City Council. One Victorian building, the old pump house, was converted into 'The Quay' public house (now a supermarket) and the remainder of the site was cleaned up for housing, landscaped open space and some commercial building. The landscaped area, designed by Brown Associates of Sheffield, was opened to the public in 1999. The river frontage was enhanced at this time and a new footbridge linking the

towpath through to Castle Gardens was added.

The Bede Island building which was constructed in 1998, is one of a set of commercial buildings designed by Stephen George & Partners and built by William Davis Ltd. along the river front as part of the major urban regeneration initiative.

(Photograph: De Montfort University)

Bede Island

(Photograph: De Montfort University)

Campus Centre

The Campus Centre on three floors was completed in 2003 and refurbished in 2016 as a state-of-the-art Student's Union building with an appropriate blend of small breakout spaces and larger social areas. Additionally the third floor provides accommodation for exhibitions, conferences, open days, examinations and particularly dance/drama activities. Various retail outlets service both staff and students of the university.

The building was located on the site of the former Stibbe Building, which had been used by the university and former polytechnic as its workshop and stores. Stibbe were a well known company in Leicester producing knitwear machinery in a number of factories. During archaeological excavations prior to building work, evidence of massive ditches associated with the town's Civil War defences of c.1640, were found in this area and under the Innovation Centre. The defences had been modified several times within a period of a few years. The building, designed by Ellis Williams Architects based in London, Warrington and Berlin, was built by Balfour Beatty and officially opened by Lord Waheed Ali in November 2003.

The building is of steel frame construction with pumped concrete floors on permanent steel formwork. Walls within the steel framework are infilled with a blend of fairfaced concrete and imported red ceramic blocks. The extended roof with a louvered façade provides a protected zone and entrance to the

building, although it is noted that sun shading is lacking on the south elevation, causing the atrium space to overheat at lunchtime in the warmer months.

The Campus Centre incorporates a full height glazed curtain wall frontage giving attractive views down the landscaped Mill Lane. The ground floor offers seating areas with bar and coffee bar facilities whilst the first floor provides accommodation for Student's Union activities.

Kimberlin Library

The Kimberlin Library was built in two main phases. The original building was opened by Mrs I.L. Kimberlin in November 1977, and named after Mr A.H.W. Kimberlin OBE FCI, who was chairman of the Leicester Polytechnic governors from 1971 to 1976 and its constituent colleges from 1956. He had been associated with the Polytechnic and former colleges since 1947, and was Lord Mayor of Leicester in 1964-65.

The Kimberlin Library was designed by the Leicestershire County Architects under Thomas Locke (County Architect) to provide full provision of library services as a central facility. This was to replace smaller subject libraries which had previously been located in different buildings around the campus. At the time of the first phase, accommodation was required for reference and loan books, also non-book media such as slides, illustrations, maps and tapes.

The four storey building was built on piled foundations with an in-situ concrete frame and waffle floor system, affording an open plan layout, suitable for the high loading associated with book stacks. The exposed internal woodwork for doors, frames, skirting, stairways etc. was Columbian Pine from sustainable forests, which was clearly forward -looking at that time. The underside of the concrete waffle floor is exposed in certain locations, where suspended ceilings were not required to hide services.

Externally the building is faced in red engineering bricks, which are

also featured in the original main staircase. The phase one plans envisaged potential extension towards the south side from the main staircase, but this option was not taken up by the second building phase, which extended across the site of the single storey exhibition hall. The building, with its vertical slit windows is rather introspective, reflecting its function of supporting a range of learning activities. Provision at ground level was made for a bookshop but this is now

accommodation for the university archive.

The second phase of the library was designed by Eva Jiricna, Architects and Atelier10, Environmental and Services Engineers in 1997 to serve the electronic revolution in library and internet media. The first proposal by the University was for an additional lightweight construction floor above the original building. However, this proved impracticable and a whole new wing was developed. The

building on four floors is of a lighter weight construction and designed to accommodate extensive computing facilities rather than heavy books. A new central core and entrance was added with disabled access, also a feature tensile fabric canopy which deteriorated rapidly and has been replaced. The main building structure is a steel frame clad in grey ceramic panels, but in contrast to the first building phase has a more extrovert appearance. The library extension completes the three-sided courtyard between the Eric Wood administrative building and the polychromatic Queen's Building. The internal environment is controlled by external shading whilst maintaining its light and airy character to serve the computer facilities and open plan study spaces.

In 2007, the original phase of the library was refurbished and modified to create easier access to the loans counter. Further enhancements in 2015 improved the entrance foyer and circulation space. Library opening hours have been extended to reflect diverse student learning patterns including the extensive use of the internet and electronic media. Additional learning zones are located in the Eric Wood and Greenhouse buildings.

PACE Performance Arts Centre

The Centre for Excellence in Performance Arts building was completed in 2007 as the National Centre for Excellence in Teaching and Learning in Performance Arts.

The building was designed by Ellis Williams Architects, who also designed the University Campus Centre. Construction was by Interserve Builders. The building is constructed on a steel frame and finished externally with white 'Sto' render system applied to particleboard, insulation and mesh.

The brief for the building required floors for music, dance and performance respectively to be interactively connected by plasma screens. Visual linkage was also required through viewing galleries.

Sprung floors were required for dance also a studio with break-out rooms for individual or small group practice and experimentation.

Prior to construction, the site, including the larger area for the new Faculty of Business and Law building, was investigated by the University of Leicester Archaeological Services who found evidence of Iron Age, Roman and medieval activity. Some evidence of Iron Age occupation was in the form of residual Iron Age pottery recovered from later features. The main Roman feature was a section of the north-south road which ran from the south gate of Roman Leicester to the small town of Tripontium on the Leicestershire-Warwickshire border. This road, dated between the second and

fourth centuries AD, had previously been identified under the Innovation Centre site in 1993.

Medieval evidence related to the suburban settlement of the 13th century, predating the 14th century New Worke (Newarke). It included the north-east Newarke wall of c.1400, evidence of earlier buildings outside this wall along Oxford Street and subsequent buildings within the Newarke religious precinct. Post-medieval archaeology showed a substantial ditch running parallel to Oxford Street, and it is suggested that this formed part of the town's Civil War defences of c.1640. More recent remains related to the 18th and 19th century buildings along Oxford Street including the barracks of the Leicestershire Regiment.

Hugh Aston Building

The Faculty of Business and Law Hugh Aston Building for the Leicester Business School and the Leicester De Montfort Law School, completed in 2009, was designed by CPMG Architects of Nottingham and built by SOL Construction Ltd., later renamed Rok Construction following a merger. It was officially opened by Patrick McKenna, Founder and Chief Executive of Ingenious Media, in March 2010. The building frames the entrance to the University Campus from the city. The landscaping scheme opens up 'Magazine Square' to create a tree-lined plaza accessible to the public and the university with the 15th century Magazine gateway as the focal point of the square directing the pedestrian route to the city centre.

The new building incorporates many energy efficient features appropriate to the early 21st century with its concerns for the environment and fuel efficiency. Natural daylight and ventilation are maximised, and thermal mass is used to reduce fluctuations of the internal temperature. A ground source is used to collect heat in the winter and provide summer cooling.

Oxford Street

Rainwater is harvested for non-potable functions. Public atriums and 'winter gardens' allow natural light and fresh air into the building. Solar array panels on the roof heat the domestic hot water system. The building was rated as 'excellent' to Building Research Establishment Environmental Assessment Method (BREEAM) criteria.

The architects CPMG formed in 1997 from the merger of Crampin & Pring and James McArtney architects have a long track record of designing pioneering buildings for the education sector, including the Universities of Sheffield, Nottingham, Nottingham Trent, Loughborough and Teesside.

Oxford Street

Magazine Square

Magazine Square

The reinforced concrete frame building, featuring glazing and pre-patinised copper cladding has a massing which reduces towards the Magazine gateway, but which frames the open spaces to the Magazine and to the front of the Hawthorn Building. The building's facilities include lecture theatres, meeting rooms, a mock law court, the faculty law library and a café.

Hugh Aston Courtyard

Mock Law Court

The site had previously been occupied by the James Went Building, built in two phases in the early 1970s. This building had become too expensive to maintain and to convert satisfactorily to give disability access. It was therefore demolished in 2004, and the site was fully investigated for deeply buried archaeological remains from early Leicester before work could commence on the new Hugh Aston Building. The site for the new building also extended over ramps formerly associated with the pedestrian underpass beneath Oxford Street, on the campus side of The Magazine. This was made possible by the realignment of Oxford Street to its original line on the east side of The Magazine.

Former James Went Building demolished in 2004

The building is named after Hugh Aston who from 1525 to 1548 was the organist and choirmaster in the Collegiate Church of St Mary of the Annunciation in the Newarke, the remains of which are in the basement of the Hawthorn Building. Hugh Aston died in 1558 having been at different times the Coroner, Mayor, Member of Parliament and Auditor of Accounts for Leicester. He also was one of England's foremost Tudor composers and head of music at the Collegiate Church and Hospital of the Newarke.

Arrival of the royal party through the Magazine Gateway;
below centre: HM The Queen and HRH The Duke of Edinburgh at the University
(Photographs: De Montfort University)

On 8 March 2012, HM The Queen accompanied by HRH The Duke of Edinburgh and HRH The Duchess of Cambridge, unveiled a plaque commemorating the start of the Queen's Diamond Jubilee Tour of the United Kingdom. The Queen and The Duchess of Cambridge attended a fashion and culture show in the Hugh Aston courtyard. HRH The Duchess of Cambridge chose a student's shoe design, inspired by 19th century fashions and Kate's engagement ring, to be made up and presented to her at a later date. The royal party entered the University campus through the Magazine Gateway to be greeted by a large crowd of staff, students and members of the public.

HM The Queen and HRH The Duchess of Cambridge
(Photograph: De Montfort University)

HM The Queen with Professor
Dominic Shellard, Vice-Chancellor
at the fashion show
(Photograph: De Montfort
University)

HM The Queen unveils the commemorative plaque on the Hugh Aston Building
(Photograph: De Montfort University)

Queen Elizabeth II Diamond Jubilee Leisure Centre

The Queen Elizabeth II Diamond Jubilee Leisure Centre built by Morgan Sindall to a design by the specialist leisure and sporting facility architects, S&P Architects opened in July 2012. S&P Architects were responsible for the detailed design of the London 2012 Olympics Aquatics Centre in association with Zaha Hadid Architects. The centre is popularly known as the 'QEII'.

The new leisure centre on the former Central Railway viaduct site, has an extensive range of sporting and health facilities, including a 25m swimming pool, sports hall, climbing wall and fitness centre.

Swimming pool and sports hall

Entrance foyer

The Queen Elizabeth II Diamond
Jubilee Leisure Centre was officially
opened on 7 June 2013 by HRH Earl
of Wessex.

Studio

Fitness centre

Vijay Patel Building

The elegant Vijay Patel building forms the centre piece of the university campus. Designed by CPMG Architects and built by Balfour Beatty as main contractor, the new £42m complex comprises three main areas. The Arts Tower, formed from the refurbished Fletcher Tower, the design wing and the catering area. In addition, the open parkland along Mill Lane reconnects the city with the River Soar through a series of linked high-quality urban spaces through the university campus. The building is the home for Art and Design within the Faculty of Arts, Design and Humanities and incorporates a large gallery space. The Vijay Patel building also houses the Centre for English Language Learning.

The Vijay Patel complex replaced the former Fletcher high and low rise accommodation, which included the 1960s student union building, art and design accommodation and the 1993 Health Centre. The new building brings together all art and design subjects and their associated workshops. The building is named after Dr Vijay Patel, a graduate of the Leicester School of Pharmacy and a major benefactor to the university.

The Confucius Institute promoting Chinese language and culture is located in a purpose-built part of the Vijay Patel Building.

The former Fletcher Building was officially opened by Her Majesty Queen Elizabeth The Queen Mother on 2nd November 1966, as an extension to the Leicester Colleges of Art and Technology. The building was designed by the Leicester City Architects' Department led by Stephen George as City Architect and built by M.J. Gleeson (Contractors) Ltd. The architectural concept was to contrast the strong verticality of the ten-storey tower with the horizontal lines of the low rise to create collegiate-style courtyards. The Fletcher Building was named after Mr Benjamin Fletcher, who was Head Master of the Art School from 1900.

Adjacent to the Vijay Patel Building is a 1982 red painted untitled sculpture by John Hoskin. The piece, popularly known as 'The Waffle' because of its grid-like elements, was originally located in front of the Eric Wood Building, but was relocated in 1992 when the Queen's Building was constructed. It had been designed to act as a visual link between the Eric Wood and original Kimberlin Library Building, but now it has visual relationships with the Vijay Patel Building and the Newark Point hall of residence.

The former Fletcher Building

Riverside Café

Untitled sculpture by
John Hoskin, 1982

The Gallery

Halls

New Wharf Hall, 1995

Bede Hall, 1998

De Montfort University owns two halls of residence, namely Bede Hall (1998) on Bede Island and New Wharf Hall (1995) built by Wimpey Construction UK Ltd. East Midlands adjacent to the new almshouse building on Western Boulevard. Additionally two halls, The Grange (1970) developed by Western Challenge Housing Association Ltd. Christchurch and Waterway Gardens (1998) developed by Derwent Living Ltd. Derby are leased by the university. The remaining halls are commercial halls but with special arrangements for housing De Montfort University students.

The Grange, 1970
(Photographs: De Montfort University)

Waterway Gardens, 1998

Commercial Halls

Commercial Halls are located around the University Campus, but not all halls are illustrated. A range of other privately owned halls also offer accommodation to De Montfort University students.

Newarke Point, 2003-2004
(Unite)

Victoria Hall, 2003
(Victoria Hall Ltd.)

Gosling Court, 2001
(Westmanor Properties Ltd.)

Kingfisher Court, 2003
(Westmanor Properties Ltd.)

The Grange, 2003
(Unite)

Filbert Village, 2003
(Unite)

Grosvenor House, 2003 (Opal Property Group Ltd.
(Photograph: De Montfort University)

Liberty Park, 2003 (Liberty Living Ltd.)
(Photograph: De Montfort University)

Bibliography

Allaway, A. J., 1962. *Vaughan College Leicester 1862-1962*. Leicester University Press.

Baker, David. 1984. *Leicester University Library, A History to 1961*, Leicester University.

Barton, Susan. 2014. *Boulevard Rink / Sandford Centre*, Private communication.

Boynton, Helen. 1993. *A Prospect of Oadby – The Story of its Northern Development from 1902 to 1992*. Leicester: Oadby Local History Group.

Boynton, Helen and Pitches, Grant. 1996. *Desirable Locations – Leicester's Middle Class Suburbs 1880-1920*. Leicester City Council.

Boynton, Helen. 2000. *The History of Victoria Park Leicester*. Leicester: Boynton.

Boynton, Helen. 2001. *The Changing Face of London Road, Leicester*. Leicester: Boynton.

Boynton, Helen. 2002. *The History of New Walk Leicester*. Leicester: Boynton.

Boynton, Helen. 2003. *Knighton and Clarendon Park. The Story of a Leicester Suburb*. Leicester: Boynton.

Boynton, Helen. 2004. *South East of Leicester*. Leicester: Boynton.

Boynton, Helen and Dickens, Keith. 2006. *Leicester and its Suburbs in the 1920s and '30s*. Leicester: Boynton.

Brandwood, Geoff and Cherry, Martin, 1990. *Men of Property – The Goddards and Six Generations of Architecture*. Leicester Museums Publication No. 107, Leicester.

Burch, Brian. 1996. *The University of Leicester – A History 1921-1996*. Leicester University Press.

Cantor, L. and Squires, A., 1997. *The Historic Parks and Gardens of Leicestershire and Rutland*. Leicester: Kairos Press, Newtown Linford.

Cavanagh, T. and Yarrington, A., 2000. *Public Sculpture of Leicestershire and Rutland*. Liverpool University Press.

Chinnery, G.A., 1981. *Leicester Castle & The Newarke*. Leicestershire Museums Publications No.19. Leicester.

Cocks, T.Y., 1997. *Leicester's Royal Foundation: The Hospital of the Holy Trinity*. Governors of Trinity Hospital, Leicester.

County Records Office. *Borough of Leicester Urban Sanitary Authority Street Index Registers of Deposited Plans*, County Records Office, Wigston, Leicester.

County Records Office. *Register of Oadby Deposited Plans*, County Records Office, Wigston, Leicester.

County Records Office. *Wright's and Kelly's Directories*. Various years, County Records Office, Wigston, Leicester.

Courtney, P., 1995. *Castle Park – A Souvenir Guide*. Leicestershire County Council.

Cunningham, S and Taylor, Alan, 1984/1987. *History of Charles Frears School of Nursing*. Unpublished paper. De Montfort University, Leicester.

De Montfort University. 1992. *Master Plan,* Livingstone Eyre Associates. De Montfort University, Leicester.

De Montfort University. 2002. *Master Plan One*, Robert Turley Associates, Birmingham.

De Montfort University. 2007. *Master Plan Two*, Asset & Infrastructure Management Solutions: Nuneaton & London.

De Montfort University. 2014. *Master Plan Three*, Robert Turley Associates, Birmingham.

Elliot, Malcolm. 1999. *Leicester - A Pictorial History*. 2nd ed. Chichester: Phillimore.

Ellis, Colin. 1948. *History in Leicester*. City of Leicester.

Felstead, A., Franklin, J. & Pinfield, L. 1993. *Directory of British Architects 1834-1900*. London: Mansell.

Gateway. *1928-1978* and *1971*.

Gateway College. *Proposed Frazer Building 1995*.

Gateway School. *Prospectus 1939*.

Gill, Richard. 1985. *The Book of Leicester*. Buckingham: Barracuda Books Ltd.

Hickman, Trevor. 2002. *The Best of Leicester*. Sutton Publishing.

Hoskins, W.G., 1950. *The Heritage of Leicester*. City of Leicester.

Hoskins, W.G., 1970. *Leicestershire*. London: Faber and Faber.

Jones, Donald. 2001. *University of Leicester, School of Education 1946-1996*. University of Leicester.

Leicester City Council. 1975. *Leicester's Architectural Heritage*. Leicester City Council.

Leicester City Council. 1990. *The Quality of Leicester*. Leicester City Council.

Leicester City Council. 2004. *New Walk Conservation Area*. Leicester City Council.

Leicester City Council. 2006. *The Castle Conservation Area*. Leicester City Council.

Leicester Mercury. 1989. *Leicester in the Fifties*. Archive Publications.

Lyons, Arthur. 2012. *The Architecture of the Universities of Leicester*. 2nd ed. Leicester. Anchorprint.

McKean, John. 1994. *Leicester University Engineering Building – James Stirling and James Gowan*. London: Phaidon.

Mee, Arthur. 1937. *The King's England – Leicestershire and Rutland*. London: Hodder and Stoughton.

Morris, Mathew and Buckley, Richard, 2014. *Richard III, The King under the Car Park*. University of Leicester.

Nichols, John, 1815. *The History and Antiquities of the County of Leicester*. Vol.I, Part II. London: Nichols, Son & Bentley.

Orme, H.G. and Brock W.H., 1987. *Leicestershire's Lunatics*. Leicestershire Museums Publications No. 87. Leicester.

Pevsner, N., 1984. *The Buildings of Leicestershire and Rutland*. 2nd ed. London: Penguin.

Qube Planning Ltd., 2005. *Oadby Hill Top & Meadowcourt Conservation Area Appraisal*.
     Borough of Oadby & Wigston, Leicester.

Ranger, William. 1851. *Report of the General Board of Health of the Burial Ground and New Cemetery of Leicester*. London.

Roberts, T., 1920. *Ancient & Historical Buildings in the Vicinity of the Portland Shoe Works Leicester*. Leicester: Staynes.

Silverman, H.A., 1930. *The Vaughan College Leicester*. University of Leicester Archives.

Simmons, Jack, 1958. *New University*. Leicester University Press.

Simmons, Jack, 1963. *Leicester and its University*. Leicester University Press.

Skillington, S.H., 1931. *The Trinity Hospital Leicester*. Leicester: Edgar Backus.

Sudjic, D., 1986. *New Directions in British Architecture - Norman Foster, Richard Rogers, James Stirling*.
     London: Thames & Hudson.

Thompson, A. Hamilton, 1937. *The History of the Hospital and the New College of the Annunciation of St. Mary in the
     Newarke, Leicester,* Leicestershire Archaeological Society. Leicester: Backus.

University of Leicester. 1993. *The History of Salisbury Road*. Friends of the Department of English Local History
     Newsletter. No.6. October 1993.

University of Leicester. 2008. *'A Hell of a Job; Building the University of Leicester'*, Lecture by Dr William Whyte.
     19 February 2008. University of Leicester.

University of Leicester. 2008. *University of Leicester Development Framework Plan 2008*.
     London: Shepheard Epstein Hunter.

University of Leicester. 2016. *Campus Guidebook*. Internal publication, University of Leicester.

Whitaker, J.H.McD., 1981. *Building Stones of Leicester – A City Trail*. Leicestershire Museums Publications No.20. Leicester.

Wills, Deryk (Ed.). 1999. *Oadby 2000*. Oadby, Leicestershire: Oadby Local History Group.

Index of Persons